Letters
From
Provence

Letters From Provence

CECILIA PHILLIPS

Illustrations by Fernand Téodil

GARNSTONE PRESS

Published for the Author by
GARNSTONE PRESS LIMITED
59 Brompton Road, London SW3 1DS
ISBN: 0.85511.232.8
© Cecilia Phillips, 1975

Printed by Anchor Press Limited,
and bound by William Brendon & Son,
Tiptree

Contents

Places Mentioned

Aigues-Mortes
Aix-en-Provence
Ajaccio (Corsica)
Albaron
Alpilles
Aramon
R. Ardèche
Arles
Aven d'Orgnac
Bagnols-sur-Cèze
Barbegal
Barbentane
Barjols
Le Barroux
Bastia (Corsica)
Les Baux
Beaucaire
Le Beaucet
Beaumes-de-Venise
Bedoin
Bellegarde
Bonifacio (Corsica)
Bonnieux
Bonpas
Bouches-du-Rhône
Boulbon
Buoux
Cabrières
Camargue
Carpentras
Cavaillon
Cévennes
R. Cèze
Châteaurenard
Comtat Venaisson
Corsica
La Crau
Dentelles de Montmirail
Drôme
R. Durance

Eyguières
Eyragues
Fontaine de Vaucluse
Fontvieille
Fos
Frigolet
Gard
R. Gardon
Glanum
Gordes
Gorges de la Nesque
Gorges du Tarn
Graveson
Haute Galine
Isle-sur-Sorgue
Javon
Joncas
Jonquières
Languedoc
Lioux
Lourmarin
Lozère
Mt. Luberon
Lussan
Maillane
Malaucène
Marseille
Martigues
Maussane
Ménerbes
Monieux
La Montagnette
Monteux
Montfrin
Montmajour
Montmoiron
Montpellier
Mouries
Nîmes
Noves

Line Drawings

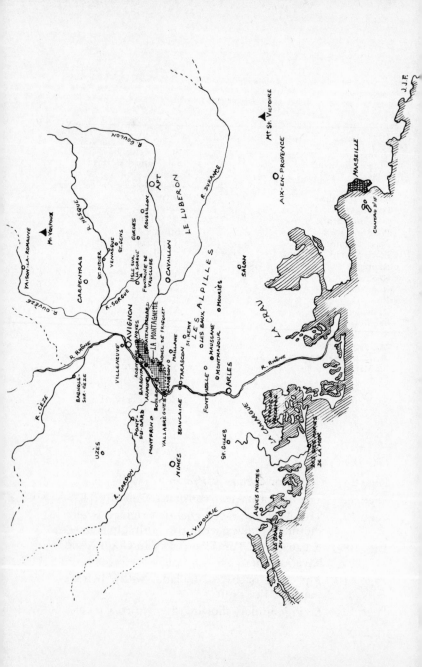

The title was that of a radio series round which this book is based. My thanks are due to *The Scotsman* for permission to include certain material originally published therein.

To Fernand
Without whose help
this book
could never have
been written

———

1. *We Bought a Mas*

Yes, we've not only bought the old tumbledown Mas but are now actually installed – a far greater achievement than it might appear on paper. We agreed with the agent, we agreed with the owners, we all trooped to their Notaire in Avignon and he, or at least his clerk, was horrified.

'You can't just buy a house like that, not even if the money's in your pocket, one has to ask Marseille.'

If someone says 'Marseille' in a context like that, he means the Préfécture, where papers are apt to disappear while Awaiting Authority. In this case Authority concerned both Urbanization and Agriculture, and our hearts sank. It reminded us forcibly of the visa necessary for our wedding. Sent from London to Paris and traced from there to Marseille, it then passed into Limbo and was never seen again. Only because Fernand luckily Knew the right sort of Someone, could we get married at all. However, this time, after some chivvying from the village Mayor (even a small village has a Mayor, who is a sort of combined Magistrate, Civil Servant and Nurse to his people) the necessary paper eventually arrived. I phoned the Notaire's clerk.

'He's out,' the receptionist replied, but I none the less began a long list of questions.

'Just a minute,' she said, 'I'll ask him.'

And, of course, there he was all the time and we got the date fixed for the sale.

If you've never seen a French Acte de Vente, you must read ours one day. It's a linguistic gem and a most amusing source of information regarding the various previous owners. Nice to know, for example, that none of them was in a 'state of interdiction', nor 'pursued by the law', nor 'touched, nor susceptible to be so by the dispositions of the decrees and orders in force concerning illicit profits and national dignity'.

I was also intrigued to learn that as the new proprietors we should allow *'les servitudes, passives, apparentes ou occultes'*. Upon inquiry, an occult servitude turns out to be only a hidden right of way. So far none such has come to light.

Once the building belonged to us, came the problem of getting the work of reconstruction under way. A friendly architect began a beautiful plan headed 'State of the Places' but his chief assistant fell into a ditch at the Fair of Beaucaire and broke his leg. The desired builders proved hard to run to earth and we spent much time, petrol and temper chasing them between Beaucaire and St. Rémy. After that we spent even more time haggling over the resultant estimate, so as to cut it to more reasonable proportions.

One recommended electrician lived in Barbentane and the other in the wilderness of hills beyond Beaucaire. We thought Barbentane would be simpler to find, but not so.

'If he's not there, he must be at his new villa,' said one of the villagers.

'And where would that be?'

'Over the little bridge, towards Avignon, but bear

right down the old route to St. Rémy. You can't miss it.'

For half an hour we missed it most successfully and then arrived to find he'd gone back to the village. His wife took the message and days later he turned up with an estimate which proved so expensive that we set forth immediately for Beaucaire.

As we had suspected, there were no roads in the hills beyond; just rough stony tracks winding up towards scattered small-holdings all owned by people of the same name. We found the electrician's aunt, his cousins and eventually his mother, but he himself was, almost inevitably, in Tarascon – from where we had started.

As for the plumber, high drama. All was fixed up nicely with a small man from down the road, when he called one evening in a great state of excitement. He couldn't, it seemed, undertake the work after all, as Someone had written an anonymous letter about him to the Tax Department. We therefore procured a more expensive replacement who didn't seem to have enemies in the Maquis; but then a message came that he Wanted To See Us. We felt the plot was thickening. Had he, too, been victim of an anonymous letter? But no, it was merely that the estimate had come out for considerably more than originally stated; and after hours of bargaining the affair was settled by the traditional drink of Pastis.

Three months after we'd signed the contract for the house, work began – and so did a long series of further complications. The fosse septique was to be at the back – at the front – the back – not at all – the back after all. The chaufferie had three different proposed positions. One wall in the house was found to be worn down to half a centimetre.

Another one was discovered to have been shoring up the oven which once baked the bread for the neighbourhood. A new metrage was needed by the Mairie; new voltage for the electricity; new soundings for the water supply. The only constant aspects were the steady rise in prices, and the Tower of Babel atmosphere, as the builders spoke a mixture of French, Provençal, Spanish and Italian.

Choosing the carrelage was a feat in itself. We saw samples of these floor tiles in Avignon, others in Arles, still more were brought to the house, and finally we were whisked off by the builder to St. Rémy to see some flooring *in situ*. Here lived three dear old spinsters, who pattered from room to room twittering about the tiles, advising which ones were the worst to clean and which didn't 'fear the dirt' – the eldest sister checking and correcting her juniors all the while. From them we learnt far more about the practical aspects of carrelage than from all the specialists put together. The tiles were chosen, the floors were laid; and six months from the time the builders began, we moved in with only some of the woodwork missing and one lonely painter still at work. About the move itself, *'toute une histoire'*, as they say here, I'll tell you another time.

2.   *The Pruner of Plane Trees*

To find our Mas you only have to come into the area and look for the largest plane tree within sight. It is a landmark for miles and always referred to by the villagers as 'That Tree'!

Unpruned for years, it towered over the house in an unbecoming and damp-making mass of shade and Something just had to be Done About it before we moved in. Impossible, however, to pay the sky-high sum required to cut the branches to roof-level, so we compromised on a trimming operation.

'Never, in all my professional experience, have I seen a platane like that,' said the pruning man. His native Italian volubility was temporarily silenced as he stood, squat and dark, gazing up at the tree. After all, it must be about 300 years old and the trunk measures six metres forty centimetres round.

'Nevertheless, we'll arrange it for you,' the little Italian assured us, as he shook hands to agree the deal. 'But never,' he repeated solemnly, 'have I seen a platane like that.'

It had been quite a treasure hunt to find this expert pruner of plane trees. As everyone we mentioned the matter to in the village said, 'I think he comes from Sernhac way. The Mayor will know, because the plane trees in the square were lopped last year.'

But as we happened to know that the long-suffering Mayor had been dragged out of his bed in the middle of the night to sort out a matrimonial crisis, we didn't think it just the moment to bother him with a plane tree, so left it for a few days. When we returned the Mayor had gone away.

'Try his cousin in the Café,' was the advice from a friend in the grocer's. 'Their large tree was cut down last year. Cables in all directions there were, but someone made a false move and there was this man hanging by his fingers cut through by the wire. He just hung there screaming and people ran away for fear, but at last somebody brought a chair for him to stand on. We gave him first-aid and I went with him myself to the hospital in Tarascon. Sernhac way he came from, but the Café will know.'

With this dramatically discouraging picture in mind we went to the Café, where the man behind the counter heard out all the explanations and request for information before replying, 'You'd better ask the Patron.'

At first the Patron wasn't much more forth-coming. 'It's not the season for cutting platanes,' he answered, dismissing the question completely.

But when he understood that, despite that, we still wanted the name of the expert, he conceded, 'I remember the man but not the name. Came from Sernhac. He's absent you see.'

'Who?' We inquired in some bewilderment.

'My son. You'll have to ask my son. He'll know.'

By this time the man at the counter had had an idea.

'You could ask at the Garage on the corner, where the plane tree comes through the roof. They're sure to know. Had the tree trimmed last year.'

The garagist was tucked snugly in his tiny office, intently studying his newspaper. He scratched his head and pondered.

'I remember the man,' he said eventually, 'but not his name. He came from Sernhac. I'll need to ask my assistant. He'll know. Where are you going now?'

Then, after we'd said we were going to call on a friend up the road, he exclaimed, 'Oh, if you're going there, ask her to ask my assistant. Very friendly they are. She'll find out for you.'

No sooner had we repeated the history to our

friend than she flung open her kitchen window and in the piercing tone used by the villagers to communicate over distances, called, 'Frédéric, Frédéric!'

To our surprise a small boy came running.

'Ask Papa to say the name of the man who cuts platanes.'

And thus at last we had the answer.

Sernhac proved to be a sleepy, attractive, far from clearly signposted village in the Gard, where after three false starts we found our professional pruner of plane trees. Here, however, it's rare to fix things at once. 'We have the time,' as he said. So we first agreed that we'd all go one day together to 'Look at the tree'.

Some weeks and several telephone calls later, there we all were looking at the tree; and two months after that there was a mountain of branches in the middle of the garden.

'Just let it dry and break it up,' the Italian called optimistically as he drove off.

Thanks to a neighbour's tractor, we finally saw the end of the branches and went back to Sernhac to pay.

'Plenty of time between now and dying for paying,' said the pruner, as he led the way into the house – much to the surprise of a young woman, who having just washed her hair was then in the middle of washing the floor. Although he only indicated casually that that was 'La Fille,' he was none the less clearly proud of the fact that his daughter could write his receipts out for him.

It was only 9.30 a.m. but politeness decreed that we should drink a glass of Italian liqueur, whose fancy bottle had, it seemed, been coveted by La Fille.

But it was still of the platane that the little man was thinking and as he raised his glass to us, he repeated reminiscently, 'Never in my life had I seen such a tree.'

3. *Removal French Style*

In effect ours wasn't one removal day but two, preceded and followed by many more of chaos. To begin with, there are no furniture removal firms in our area. People here don't frequently change homes and when they do they find a friend with a lorry and call in all the neighbours to help. This simplified, though nowadays illegal, solution couldn't cope with our scattered belongings, so we came to terms with a firm from Arles. Only by agreeing to pack all the books and household as well as personal linen ourselves, could we lower the astronomical figure required. But two complications put me behind with these preparations – a frozen pipe and a gas leak.

One doesn't expect pipes to freeze in the Midi but the one bringing water from the road into the house suddenly froze good and hard. With British logic, I presumed that either the plumber could fix the matter or that the Water Authorities would Do Something. The plumber, however, said that as the trouble was outside, it wasn't his affair and the Authority (whose title can strangely be translated as Waters and Sea Air) said that pipes don't usually

freeze in the Midi and that if they do one must just
Wait for the Thaw.

This meant that half the town was Waiting for the
Thaw but nobody official seemed to mind. After
Waiting a week, we made elaborate arrangements to
bring water via a system of hosepipes across the roof
– and then of course the thaw came. We thereupon
turned our attention to the persistent smell of gas
from the cooker; but, up to the day before the move,
promises to come and deal with it had not borne
fruit.

As the removal men were due on the Thursday
morning at seven-thirty, Wednesday afternoon
became eleventh hour for the cooker and I abandoned a pile of last minute ironing to go in search of
the missing workman. He was out but after hearing
about his wife's recent illness, and drinking a
home-made liqueur to her better health, I left with
yet another promise. When I turned back into our
road what should be blocking it but the removal van.

Before I could decide whether it was the liqueur
or just a coincidence that somebody else was moving, three men came to meet me.

'We thought it would be better if we began today,'
explained the leader laconically.

Better for them perhaps but not for me because
Fernand, blissfully unaware of what was happening,
was over at the Mas and, as you know, the house had
four floors.

'Would Madame just move the coats?' (ground
floor)

'Would Madame just explain about the un-
completed packages of linen?' (first floor)

'Would Madame just finish putting the books into
the containers?' (third floor)

Meantime on the second floor all Madame wanted to do was finish the ironing. But no. 'Would Madame kindly remove everything that might be required from the kitchen for supper or breakfast, food and utensils?'

I was thus surrounded by food, utensils and ironing when the bell rang.

'I've come as promised,' smiled the man for the cooker.

Thursday dawned and having abandoned the house to the men and dumped the sheets on the window sill of the still unopened laundry, we came out to the Mas in a howling Mistral. The wind whipped the dust and builders' débris into a tornado and something went into Fernand's eye. Whether it was a splinter of glass we don't know, but he had to drive back to town with one hand covering the eye.

At the house more pastis and beer seemed to have been consumed than furniture loaded, so we took time to go to the chemist. Much to the interest of quickly gathered spectators, he sat Fernand down on a chair by the door, peered into the eye, said he could see nothing and administered some drops.

By the time we got to the house in the village where we were to have lunch, not only the eye but the face was swollen and poor Fernand could do no more. But villagers hereabouts are still able to cope with such contingencies. Quickly taking her shawl and headscarf, our hostess went off to see if a certain lady was in. Luckily she was and came straight away. With a deliberate movement she passed her wedding ring across the eyeball (I half expected to hear an accompanying incantation) and, voilà, all was well. Apparently there is another good soul in the village who deals with displaced nerves in an equally efficacious and unorthodox fashion.

Meanwhile the unloading was in full swing. The nearer it came to knocking off time, the more feverish the activity. Even the boss and his teenage son came to help. Packing-up which had taken hours, was undone with speedy and enthusiastic abandon and things dumped wherever a space could be found. The result was an interesting and frustrating sort of inverted Pelmanism: it took us two days, for example, to find the three parts (in three totally different places) of the coffee percolator used last thing on the Thursday morning.

After a final pastis and hefty tips all round ('not obligatory,' said the boss, 'but . . .'), we were left as darkness fell in the midst of utter confusion.

'Take you at least a month to sort that out,' the boss remarked cheerfully as he pocketed the cheque. We had Been Moved in true French style.

4. *Sunstruck Material*

How right you are about the curtains! With all these many curious and differently shaped windows the problem of curtaining loomed large on my daily agenda for weeks. So long as one takes plenty of time over the selectioning, there are some excellent bargains to be had from the merchants of material who sell in the weekly markets and I bought quite a lot this way. But as we wanted something better for the big sitting-room, I decided to visit Souleiado.

Souleiado is the Provençal for Sun-struck and aptly describes the hand-printed material produced by a small firm in Tarascon – the only such works left in France. The approach, between the tall, grey houses of the narrow Rue Proudhon, must be almost the same as two centuries ago when the firm was founded. By the arched entrance a metal plaque shows the name of Monsieur Charles Deméry, to whose family the works have always belonged, and across the wisteria scented courtyard I found the shop.

When the Manageress understood that I was not only interested in making curtains but also in hearing about the hand-printing process, she unrolled a bale of material to reveal the stamp: 'Souleiado. Impressions de Provence.'

'Beware of imitations!' she said adamantly, shaking her finger to emphasize the warning. 'Villains, some shopkeepers. Buy stuff from cheap factories and pass it off as the genuine thing. Always insist that they let you read the mark of the maker down the side. If they won't, it means it's not there.'

I was privately pondering the number of admittedly good imitations I had seen, when the Manageress asked if I'd like to go up to the workrooms. Beside the staircase hung an old notice advertising the ancient Provençal process of 'Imagiers de Tissu' – or the Creation of Pictures on Material, another very apt description of the resulting product.

There are 4,000 basic traditional patterns, many 300 years old, and it is the interplay of these motifs which is the concern of the design office at Souleiado. Once a new pattern has been arranged, a piece of paper, bearing what looks to the outsider like some obscure mathematical problem, is sent down to the colour and printing departments – each line of figures representing the numbers on the traditional blocks to be used in sequence.

The material is not made on the premises but arrives as long rolls of white cotton, silk or linen, ready for the dyes which brew, like some strange witch's soup, mixed with gum from Arabia. After dyeing, the material is festooned outside to dry in a courtyard as gay as the dyeworkers' quarters of the Souk in Marrakech.

Any one pattern may need as many as seven different colours; if so, it will take about two hours to hand-print one metre. The background of every design is black and I found a white-haired Monsieur hard at work on this job – not the slightest trace of join showing as he deftly moved the wooden blocks along the row.

'I'm the grandfather here in every sense,' he told me. 'I'm older than all the rest and I've worked here the longest – thirty-five years to be exact.'

He turned over the block to show me the pattern of nails fixed into the wood underneath.

'Some of the older ones have raised wooden pegs instead of the nails,' he explained, 'and some have become so worn that we can no longer use them.'

Three other members of Monsieur's family work in the same room. His son-in-law was super-imposing blue grapes onto the old man's original black design. Beside his bench stood a vat of blue dye, covered with felt so that just enough liquid seeped through ready for use. In practised rhythm, he dipped his block into the blue tint, placed it on the next strip of pattern, tapped it smartly two or three times – and there were the blue grapes neatly in place on the black trellis.

When all the colours are completed, the cloth is subjected to steam and then hung out to dry, but of course with such close work errors of judgement can occur, so the finished material is then graded into three classes. Depending where the slight fault lies, one can strike very lucky with the second and third class material – but the first-class is completely top quality, with not the least imperfection.

A further flight of stairs led to the rooms where several women were busy cutting and sewing. Although most of the material is marketed in lengths, a few ready-made articles, particularly bags, purses and mats, are stitched here. In this room, too, the workers were all old-timers (the youngest had been there nine years) and proud to feel part of the family concern.

Both the articles thus made and the material lengths are sold not only in the shop downstairs and its larger counterparts in Avignon and Paris, but also in Italy, Belgium, America, Denmark, Germany, Switzerland and, yes, England too. But just remember before you buy some Sunstruck material for your next lot of curtains: Beware of imitations, and insist on seeing that mark down the side, 'Souleiado. Impressions de Provence'!

5. *Real Cows*

'REAL cows? REAL milk?' queried our friend from across the Alpilles in tones of disbelief. She, too, is installed in the country but the only liquid milk she sees is the bottled or cartoned kind, which is so full of unreal additions that it can stay unharmed on the grocers' shelves for weeks. The nearly inevitable cycle of any area where the temperatures rise to our summer heights is – no rain, no grass, no cows, no milk.

Here, however, we have the great good fortune to have five cows belonging to a Mas not too far from ours. A ten-minute walk down the narrow lane past fruit trees and vines leads to what is known as the Quarter of the Burnt Mill. Goodness knows in what year it was burnt: there have certainly been no remaining signs of same for a very long time.

At all events, there live five nameless cows and every evening at six o'clock their milk is sold in the spotlessly scrubbed dairy by a pretty dark-haired girl. When I remarked that in England cows often have names, she replied sweetly, 'That must be because there are mountains there. I'm told that in the mountains the people name their cows.' I asked what breed of cows they were. She looked surprised that there could be more than one kind of cow and said, 'You'd have to ask my father.'

For occasionally it is her father who leaves his game of Boules in the courtyard to come and serve. As he says, 'An occupation like ours continues every day – feast days, Sundays, all are the same.' Every day, too, at half-past seven, the churn containing the results of the morning's milking (each cow yields ten litres a day) is carried to the village to stand in a shop called A Thousand Articles; so sometimes we take our bottle there to be refilled instead.

Although it is admittedly an extraordinary chance to have come to a Mas within short distance of real milk, it was even more extraordinary when we lived in Tarascon. For there, too, believe it or not, are real cows living right in the middle of the town. What's more there are no less than fourteen of these anachronistic creatures, so that a considerable number of people converge in their direction twice a day.

Personally I used to prefer the evening, when there is an almost clandestine air about the proceedings, especially in winter when darkness has already fallen. If you'd like to make an imaginary visit, rinse out your bottle and follow me.

First we cross the main boulevard where normal life bustles busily by and the road is slash-lit by the fierce illuminations of Monoprix. Then we go under an aged archway where all is suddenly still and pass the house which always has a little line of washing strung across its half-opened door.

This is the Street of the Golden Arm which, so the notice adds, leads to the Girls' School. The proximity of students and cows has caused some famous disputes but, after all, cows are feminine too and, qu'est ce que vous voulez, one must expect smells in the summer heat.

By now we have become part of an irregular procession of men, women and children carrying diverse receptacles from old lemonade bottles, via cannisters, to any saucepan free and seized at the last minute.

Thus we all approach this corner of the country in the centre of the town. For another archway then leads directly into the farmyard of an old Mas just like any in the country here, with its pots of flowers, its rabbits, cats, dogs, pigeons and hens, and the all-important cows themselves in the furthest of the many barns.

At the corner of the farmyard is an austere, cell-like structure where the elderly patronne dispenses the milk with due gravity. On one wall hangs the licence, on another the price-list and, surprising among this Carthusian-like severity, there is also a magazine picture of a typical young French girl.

The square stone table on which the churns stand could as well be some ritualistic altar – for here all is solemn and one has the feeling of assisting at a long-established rite. The steady rhythm of the dipping ladle and the ensuing swish of the warm white liquid casts a spell of silence on all who enter from the night air. There is little of the usual chatter of the Midi and even the children talk in whispers.

But in the morning light Madame is more communicative and shows a sense of dry humour. One unusually cold day for Provence, I asked about the cows. 'Oh they keep each other warm,' she said. Flu was rampant at the time and Madame screwed up one eye in the semblance of a wink as she added that, although she'd heard that a dog had caught the virus, so far the cows were keeping well.

She talked of the old days when her husband was alive and forty-five cows paraded daily through the streets to their pasturage.

'But with all this traffic today it's impossible to let them move from here,' she said. 'There are only the fourteen left now, but it's still hard work, you know.'

Yes, it's a work, but as long as it continues something of the pastoral past lingers on in Tarascon town; and here in the country we kernel a certain cachet so long as our friends can exclaim, 'REAL cows! REAL milk!'

6. *Water*

If we are lucky to have nearby cows, we are luckier still to have an excellent supply of pure water. Nobody seems to know whether it's an infiltration from the Rhône or from the Durance. We don't really care so long as it's there. Whichever way you look at it, it's a miracle of nature. Rhône or Durance, both are nowadays nasty dirty rivers but by dint of travelling through underground gravel beds the water arrives here as if from a mountain stream. It was only super carefulness for the sake of our visitors that caused us to part with the necessary fifty francs to have it analysed. It tastes good and is cool, washes the linen whiter than in soap powder advertisements and is unlimited in supply.

This is in fact remarkably fortunate, for water is always an important topic in Provence and when the summer sun beats mercilessly down on the parched lands, it looms even larger in conversation. One hears of villagers having to buy water; of the spring by an old Mas drying up for the first time; of wells that suddenly become useless, and of foreigners who build without considering the water supply first and have to move out.

There are still many houses even in the towns which have no running water and it's only a matter of a very few years since everyone in this village had to carry supplies from the street pumps. But then if that's all you've ever been used to, I suppose you don't really mind. When we bought this Mas there were no taps in or outside the house – just the pump, albeit with motor, in the barn – whereas it has proved quite easy to install a complete sanitary system.

We heard a story recently which shows not only how jealously knowledge of the whereabouts of water in some districts may be guarded but also how seriously the people of the Midi still take their disagreements. Although blood vendettas are now very rare, a family or inter-family feud can continue for years. (Even Fernand is the go-between for two sides who Never Speak.)

On the occasion mentioned, it was two men of the Alpilles, living some little way apart, who had quarrelled. Many years after the dispute had taken place, the well of the one farm dried up and the owner was obliged to move away and sell his house at a ruinously low price, because of the lack of water. No sooner had the new proprietors arrived, than the other old man paid them a neighbourly visit, in the course of which the subject of water inevitably cropped up.

'Water!' snorted the old man, 'there's plenty of water here.'

The newcomers, surrounded by barren land, looked at him in amazement. Then he explained that their property bordered the hidden Roman aqueduct which carried water from the lake.

'A little bit of digging and voilà!' he concluded.

He was of course right, although he had kept this information from his unfortunate neighbour. In addition to the house now having an ample water-supply, there is a swimming-pool in the garden!

High drama may surround the installation of a water system. After years of talking and waiting, the pipes were recently laid all the way up the Montagnette to the Abbey of Frigolet. Each completed section was a triumph to be reported in detail. Alas! When all was ready the water only flowed to one section of the buildings: the water-tower (nicely called a Château d'Eau) had, after all, been built too low.

In former years the people of Graveson carried a statue of their local patron, St. Anthime, up to Frigolet in April, while asking him to arrange for rain. If none came, the irate villagers dipped the offending saint's effigy into a ditch. On the other hand, if too much rain resulted, Graveson had a second saint ready to be interceded: St. Aureille, concerned with the wind. Today both saints seem to be out of fashion, for there is a notice in the local paper stating that the water supply to the village is to be cut off during the installation of drains.

Where once processions provided country folk with their few outings, nowadays most people have cars and there is a weekend surge towards the sea and inland places which have water for their attraction. Foreign visitors, too, collect on the banks of the Rhône and the Gardon – especially at the famous Pont du Gard – and at the Fontaine de Vaucluse, where the Sorgue rises from underground.

In fact it is often disappointing to go in summer to this beauty spot where Petrarch pined for Laura. Better by far in spring, when the green water leaps in full spate over the boulders. Evening light is best for an unhurried visit which, ideally, includes fresh trout for dinner in one of the restaurants by the bridge.

Less frequented places on the same river are Le Thor and Isle-sur-Sorgue. By its banks at Le Thor stands an early thirteenth-century church with impressive gothic vaulting. All the same, I've never quite been able to swallow the lyrical quotation from Camus which has been placed in the porch.

By way of contrast, there is a rococo church at Isle-sur-Sorgue, the place sometimes called the Venice of Provence. Fingers of the river divide the streets, and water wheels churn in unexpected corners. The Isle is a small provincial town, with tall, old-fashioned houses and obscure cafés. We find it pleasant to sit there while watching the leisurely life of Provence pass by and talking, as often as not, of water.

7. *Candles and Cannis*

I'm so glad you liked the candles. They are made in the village of Graveson, on the eastern side of the Montagnette, by a small family business which keeps going despite pressure from larger firms.

When we entered the low building which houses this candle-making concern, there was an overpowering, though not unpleasant, smell. Monsieur le Propriétaire came to greet us and, laughing at our wrinkled noses, he explained that this smell of melted wax has always been the background to his life; for his father used to be the lay manager of the candle-making works owned by and situated at the

Premonstratensian Abbey of Frigolet. I remembered having been in the former Ciergerie at
Frigolet – a house of small rooms and stone floors,
now occupied by two retired nuns of the Order.

When the Religious Orders were driven from
France in 1903, the former manager bought the
business and moved it to Graveson. But, as most of
the custom came from the churches, he kept the
name; and thus more than half a century since the
monks ceased to own it, we still walked into the
'Ciergerie des Prémontrés'.

At first glance it looked like some genial witch's
den. Six workers, all local and long-serving (one of
the women ever since she could remember) were
manoeuvering a strange assortment of weights, pul-
leys, iron-spikes, barrels and cauldrons. A cheerful
man stood on a tressel throwing scoopfuls of soft
white substance over a round mould, like icing-
sugar over some exotic cake.

Gradually, with the aid of a patient girl worker,
we began to understand what was going on. She
showed us how with a pulley she dipped a ring of
iron-spikes into a vat of melted wax. At first nothing
could be seen but twenty-five dips gave sufficient
coating for a thin candle. The barrels were for rol-
ling tapers and the cauldrons contained different
waxes, white wax substitutes and pure yellow bee
wax. (An altar candle must contain at least thirty per
cent of pure wax.) And then of course there were
the novelty candles shaped in pyramids and vari-
ously coloured like the ones we sent to you. Curiously enough, these are sold by weight.

All the mixing and vapour-heating is supervised
by Monsieur himself and it is he, too, who sees to the
great oil boiler which burns all night. Furthermore,

his are the tasks of ordering, checking, storing, packing and dealing with correspondence. Time-consuming and tiring work, yet, with innate courtesy, he put all aside for two casual callers.

What is more, the average tourist to the region simply refuses to believe that people in Provence do anything but an absolute minimum of work. The other day as we stood on the hillside below Les Baux we overheard one visitor from the North enthusing, 'There's air, there's sun, there's everything one needs.' And he went on to comment on the number of men seen in cafés playing cards in an afternoon.

Presumably he was too stupified by the sun and the cigales to realize that those same men in the cafés were almost certainly already working in the fields

well by five o'clock in the morning. It is easy to over-glamorize life in Provence but life is as full of toil and problems here as elsewhere. Perhaps it is that the people, also mellowed by the sun, tend to accept the inevitable more philosophically.

It was particularly ironical to have heard this typical tourist's reaction just then, for only a few minutes later we heard another voice expressing a totally different point of view.

'What's to be done? One has to go on. It's necessary to earn one's living.'

This was a Monsieur of Maussane in the Alpilles to whom we had gone to buy stakes for the garden. Recently both his wife and son died but with only the aid of an apprentice he struggles to continue his family business of cane-wear. Cannis, as they are known locally, or Cannes de Provence, are the bamboo type plants which grow in the hedgerows and are bound together for fencing and windbreaks against the Mistral.

That may sound easy but it takes a craftsman to complete the job, and this Monsieur is one. Most of his cannis come from the Gard and stand stacked behind the workshop in pyramids, forming a mock African village.

Nowadays the staples are fixed by machine but the measuring is still done by eye. The fan-belt used when the canes are cut is so precious to Monsieur that he brings it from the shed and positions it himself. It is only by taking such care that small craftsmen can earn enough money for the daily round. Yet when a Swiss couple came for an ordered fence and found that they couldn't pay, Monsieur waived their excuses away saying, 'One mustn't make bad blood over money.'

It is this calm philosophy and the determined continuing of tradition, rather than the air and sun, which gives the charm to life in Provence.

8. Scorpions, Snakes and Scolopandres

There's no good denying that there are scorpions, for you'd be sure to meet one the day you arrived – not, so far as I know, that any of our visitors have done so yet. In fact scorpions are much less in evidence than when we first came, as they had then had free run of all the old stones and plaster for the two years that the house had been empty. In any case, the scorpion of Provence is a very miniature and relatively harmless variety. Also, if you knock one to the ground it invariably stays still for a moment, making it easy to deal with.

Snakes? Never, well hardly ever. The tiniest, thinnest one imaginable once wriggled its way across the drive, flicking its tongue in and out with rapid apprehension when it spotted us. As we approached nearer, it coiled up and we put a glass jar over the top while inspecting the marks. Given the all clear (for it was just a minute Couleuvre, completely harmless), it disappeared with extraordinary speed. Now that the gravel has been spread, it's most unlikely that we'll see another.

Not that one ever knows. I shall certainly never

forget the first time I met a snake in Provence – when I was staying alone in the cottage at Haute Galine. At the time I was reading 'A Wayfarer in Provence' by E. I. Robson, written in 1926, which has the passage: 'You cannot be a mere hustling tourist in Provence. Something of the mystic must be about you, if you are not to go away cold and empty.'

I remember looking out of the window at the long line of cypresses rising like black flames against the background of the Alpilles. Cypress, almonds, olives, vines have for centuries aroused the deep thoughts from which spring the myths and legends of mystical mankind: and all are woven into the background of Provence.

Turning from the window and from the poetical to the practical aspect of trees, I put some more wood in the kiln-shaped fireplace and, settling into the corner where the mule was once stabled, I reflected wryly that there was also something mystical about the workings of Provençal electricity, when a fire can be needed not for warmth but for light. The electrician, pipe in mouth, gesticulated helplessly each time he came.

'Qu'est ce qu'il faut faire?' he said, using the expression common when something is beyond control.

'Qu'est ce qu'il faut faire?' indeed, or, 'De que fo fare?' as it comes in Provençal, when it wasn't the Electricity of France but the local Mairie who had decided the current power.

Suddenly I heard a whispering sound behind me. Nobody there. Getting altogether too fanciful, I told myself, and threw another log on the fire. But the whisper came again, as the flame shot up to reveal the sinuous shape of a sizeable snake slithering across the floor.

As it happened, I had already been shattered that day by another first encounter. A Scolopandre, the only poisonous form of centipede in the area – an awesome creature with scaly armour and horns – had ensconced himself in the sink. Being a coward, I left him there and did the washing up in the bathroom. (For your consolation, Fernand, born and bred Provençal, has never seen a Scolopandre.)

The sight of the snake galvanized me out of the southern attitude of *laissez faire*. But it lay writhing round a table leg between me and the bedroom where I needed to change from slacks and espadrilles into skirt and sandals before I could go to fetch help. Even in an emergency one observes decorum in the country. So I threw the hearth mat onto it – much to its hissing indignation. Then it placed itself between me and the front door. I hurled lampshades, papers and books until it retreated under a chair. Out with a failing torch on the darkest night possible, until I reached the nearest Mas.

The next hazard was the dogs (every Mas has at least one and often two or three guard dogs), which set up a fearsome baying. In the blackness I couldn't see whether or not they were chained but as I hesitantly waved my pin-point torch, the old lady from the Mas called, 'Who's there?'

Following her came the rest of the household, led by her son Marius, and a visitor. I explained my arrival.

'*Tiens*. That makes an impression,' exclaimed a young woman.

'I think I should have been rigid with fear,' said the older one, slapping her thigh resoundingly at the idea.

But the men laughed. 'It must have been a lizard you saw.'

Nevertheless they agreed to come and look and when they saw the disorder and no snake they laughed again – until Marius moved the wood pile and the creature slithered out.

'It was a snake after all,' he allowed as he dispatched it with a blow on the head; only afterwards adding, 'but that kind isn't poisonous.'

From the kitchen he returned with the Scolopandre and remarked, 'Now he is dangerous, that one.'

'*Coquin de bon soir!*' exclaimed the visitor. 'This isn't a house: it's a zoo.'

Needless to say, the story was soon being enjoyed all round Haute Galine and as everyone who heard it said, 'It's so rare for a snake to get into a house. The mystery is, how did it enter?'

And I smiled to myself, remembering how Robson had laid it down that in Provence, 'Something of the mystic must be about you.'

9.   Bagnols and Beyond

Thank you for remembering our Wedding Anniversary. We had a good day out, including an unexpected visit to the picture gallery in Bagnols-sur-Cèze. On every previous occasion we'd driven through the town we had wanted to stop and see the pictures but there had never been time. Yesterday, not having expected to be in Bagnols at all, we not only managed to stop but arrived just at the right moment to be of some use to its curator.

'That presents us with a problem,' we heard him saying in a worried tone of voice. He ruffled his white hair, stroked his chin and emphasized, 'That indeed presents us with a problem.'

Drama lies latent under all situations in the Midi and we couldn't resist drawing nearer to find out what this grave problem could be. But needless to say it wasn't so grave as all that. A determined American visitor wanted to pay with a Travellers' Cheque for a twelve franc reproduction of a Renoir, and she was absolutely astounded that there could still be somewhere in the world where neither a cheque nor even hot dollars would be gratefully received in the middle of a Sunday afternoon.

However when I explained that the sum concerned was only twelve francs and not twelve hundred, she found she had the change after all and swept off down the stairs, followed by a harassed looking chauffeur who was most relieved at not having had to forward the money himself.

The curator was also grateful to find his problem so satisfactorily resolved and he chatted willingly about the pictures he guards in this museum founded by Leon Alègre in 1850: the first provincial museum to be established in France. In 1918 the painter Albert André took over both its direction and development.

'André and Renoir were great friends, you see,' he explained. 'They spent hours together in Alègre's garden and that's how we come to have so many of Renoir's paintings and sketches. For the rest . . .' he indicated amongst the many other works those by Monet, Manet, Pissaro, Boudin, Rodin and Gauguin . . . 'gifts, gifts. Sometimes the State; but we have been fortunate in receiving many gifts.'

Good fortune for the people of Bagnols and for visitors who find their way to see these treasures so happily displayed in their outmoded and therefore authentic surroundings. For the rooms form part of the ancient town hall set along one side of the impressively arcaded main square, from which radiate the narrow cobbled alleys of old Bagnols.

Picturesque it may be but impracticable for modern life, so during the last few years a new Bagnols has sprung up to meet the exigencies of the nearby Atomic Station of Marcoule. Its schools are now among the most progressive in France and already the Natural History section of the museum has been rehoused in the Lycée. Doubtless eventually the paintings will also be moved and doubtless they will in some way gain. But something will also be lost when they can no longer be seen in their more natural surroundings and also when the visitor is no longer greeted at the top of the creaking stairs by a curator so devoted to his charges and their history.

We had not in fact set out to visit any museum but to fish in the river Cèze near St. Jean de Marvejols, some forty kilometres away from Bagnols; but the water had proved too low. Nevertheless we spent a pleasant and fascinating morning watching the surviving fish, which had forcibly come together in a pool formed by the inflow of a stream from the hills by the pinnacled village of Tharaux.

St. Jean de Marvejols is placed on a plateau to which one climbs steadily from Lussan, on the road from Uzès. It is a place of narrow streets and grey houses, gladdened by flowers and clearly affiliated to the Cevennes rather than Provence. We had a satisfactory lunch at a small restaurant which had also been chosen as a meeting place for a team of footballers from the Camargue. I don't know why we should have been surprised to have seen them there, any more than they to see us. In fact all roads in the direction of the Cevennes usually have a stream of cars with southern number plates, driving northwards to get their owners cool; while people from the north hurry south in search of heat. Such is the law of averages – but with changing temperatures all round these days, everyone is apt to be disappointed.

Having failed to fish in the Cèze, we then went on to try the river Ardèche but the water situation was the same. Thus we had to be content with marvelling anew at the Pont d'Arc, a natural bridge formed by the river wearing its gradual way through a wall of rock.

Fewer tourists congregate there than at that better known phenomenon of the area, the Aven d'Orgnac, where immense caves are full of grotesque stalactites and stalagmites. It takes an hour (and quite a lot of francs) to visit these but people like us who can't afford either the time or the money can still enjoy a stroll in the encircling woods – and there is even a convenient hole which looks down onto the grotto below.

This is a brown, dark-green countryside of oaks and corks, myrtles and lavender, dry stone walls and the vines of Vivarais on the way down to Pont St. Esprit. Like the famous bridge of Avignon, the Pont St. Esprit was built in the thirteenth century by a Brotherhood of Bridge Builders, who had placed themselves under the protection of the Holy Spirit. Hence the name of this rather dull and sprawling town through which we finally drove to reach Bagnols; from where, incidentally, we buy our oil made from crushed grape pips. But the factory was shut and the museum open – and that's how we found the picture gallery with its gallant curator at Bagnols-sur-Cèze.

10.   The Province of Rome

I'm sorry your friends won't be able to visit us on their way to St. Tropez. Moreover I'm not just conventionally sorry, because I really regret what they are missing. To think of Provence as the last part of France through which one rushes to reach the Côte d'Azur, is to miss out on an experience – and also, in a way, to belittle a great area of historical dignity. After all, Provence was THE Province of Rome.

In response to an appeal by the people of Marseille, the Legionaries of Sextius arrived in 123 B.C. to help repel the Celts and, attracted by the thermal springs, which continue to flow today, stayed to found Aix (Aquae Sextiae – Waters of Sextius).

The next threat came some twenty years later from the Teutons but they too were overcome by the Roman soldiers, led this time by Marius. The strategic position of the hill afterwards called Mount Sainte Victoire (the hill which so attracted Cézanne) was a decisive point in the victory, which only came after a terrible battle.

At least 100,000 Teutons were said to have been killed and as many taken prisoner. Worse still, when the men began to flee, their women made a line to turn back or kill escaping warriors. Finally, when they saw that further effort would be futile, they strangled their children before committing suicide themselves.

Many boys in Provence are even now called after the victorious Marius, (it is Fernand's second name) but it was Caesar Augustus who, towards the end of the first century B.C. made the decision to develop the region as the Provincia Romana. He gave the lands round Nîmes to the veterans of his Egyptian campaign – which explains why the town's arms include a chained crocodile.

Nîmes was then called Nemausus, the Gauls' name for the god of the spring round which they had built their settlement. The Romans, ever attracted by water, made this spring the centre of an area which included a theatre and a temple to Diana. Today in the Garden of the Fountain the remains of this temple can still be seen and, a little further on, the Tour Magne, which was once the citadel. But the best known temple of Nîmes is the so-called Maison Carrée, which while standing surprisingly in the centre of the busy modern streets, so clearly shows the Greek influence in its design.

The arena at Nîmes was built about the same time and almost to the same dimensions as that at Arles. By standards of most Roman arenas these were small, seating only about 21,000 spectators, but the one at Nîmes is the best preserved in Provence.

The most remarkable reminder of past Nîmes is of course the far-famed Pont du Gard, which was part of the long aqueduct bringing drinking water from the springs near Uzès, and to which no picture postcard can do justice. Built in the final years B.C. this mighty dry-stone bridge spans the River Gardon, its three tiers of varying sized arches providing the visual interest intended by the architect for Roman eyes. While our two Canadian nieces were over, they insisted on us all walking through the covered part in the middle, but I still prefer the view from up river.

When the Roman preoccupation with water was focussed on Arles, it resulted not only in the biggest baths of Provence being built by Constantine in the

fourth century A.D., but also, long prior to that, in running water for the public toilets, which were constructed in white marble. Between such arrangements and those of today there is too often an unfortunate difference.

Arles was taken over by Augustus and made into a capital after he had crushed Marseille, on which the town had previously been economically dependent. The Necropolis, or Alyscamps, and the theatre were two of the most outstanding features of this lovely Roman city – and they still are. Incidentally, during the summer festivals the theatre (built for 7,000 spectators) is again filled to capacity.

However the theatre at Orange, also dating from the Augustus epoch, is the best extant example in Provence. Augustus gave this former Celtic township of Arausio to the Legionaries who had fought successively against the Gauls at Marseille – which is why the Arc de Triomphe depicts the victory. It's strange to think that at the height of its Roman prosperity the town of Orange contained almost four times its present population.

Another Celtic stronghold taken over by the Romans was the place which became known as Vaison-la-Romanine. Extensive excavations have made it possible to wander again along columned streets and through the once busy shopping centre.

As beautifully situated and even, in my mind, more interesting are the excavations at Glanum outside St. Rémy. In the early days of his reign, Augustus extracted the profitable city of Glanum from the Greeks, so that this is one of the few archaeological sites in France where one can study the ruins of both Greek and Roman buildings side by side. The Municipal Arch, which stands so grandly outside the former city gates, dates from the time of Augustus' arrival at the end of the first century B.C., and it's probable that the adjacent Mausoleum was raised as a memorial to his adopted grandsons who died so young.

While these are the most important centres of Roman occupation in Provence, there are so many other less known, and sometimes as yet unexcavated, places that it's impossible to list them all here to tell your friends. Just to mention a few, there's the site of Ernaginum behind the chapel of St. Gabriel near St. Etienne du Grès; the aqueduct and mill of Barbegal; the numbers of quarries still showing traces of Roman working – and even the field between here and Tarascon where the remains of a Gallo-Roman settlement were accidentally discovered.

In effect, once people begin to look, instead of rushing by, they can scarcely help coming across some part of the ancient dignity of Provincia Romana – THE Province of Rome.

11. Honey of the Alpilles

Do you remember the old couple of Eyguières about whom Alphonse Daudet wrote in the *Lettres de Mon Moulin*? Today, a century later, we've met two similar old folk living in St. Rémy, on the other side of the Alpilles from Eyguières.

Daudet found his aged pair by taking them the

letter from his friend Maurice and by following the
instructions which the latter had sent. We found
ours by following a faded arrow under a hand-
written cardboard notice reading, *'Mie des Alpilles.'*

Normally we buy our honey from people in the
village who have hives on the Montagnette but an
occasional change of flavour whets the appetite, so
we crossed the courtyard and came into a garden
very much like the one Daudet described. Like him,
too, we found the door of the house slightly ajar; but
thought it best none the less to knock.

'Entrez, donc!' came a distant voice, so we pushed
open the door and turned into the small kitchen,
where a wizened old man was sitting by a white-
haired lady in a wheel-chair.

'Tiens!' he cried, getting up to receive us with all
the enthusiasm shown to Alphonse by the grand-
parents of Maurice. Both pleased and surprised that
someone had followed his notice about the Miel, he
shuffled into the remise and returned with a kilo of
dark-brown honey.

'You can taste it if you wish,' he said, but we
assured him we could see it was good and asked him
if he'd been an apiculturist for long.

'All my life, until three years ago when the
tragedy struck', he answered indicating the wheel-
chair. 'Three years she's been like that'.

We murmured sympathy and his wife took up
the tale.

'Both legs amputated. Just like that. Whoosh!
Previously we worked together but now here we sit
and my daughter-in-law tends the bees. *Qu'est ce que
vous voulez?* There's always something when one
becomes old.'

'Eh, oui, Qu'est ce que vous voulez?' echoed her hus-

band, and they were both resigned and accepting.

We asked about the bees and learned that their sixty-five hives have been on the Alpilles for as long as the old folk could remember, each hive housing thousands of bees. In a good year there can be three honey harvests, but more often there are only two. 'A good year' in Provence means one with rain; for vegetation soon withers in the scorching sun, and without the flowers how can bees make honey? We wondered if a better financial return could be made by selling the combs.

'*Ma foi, non!*' said Monsieur. 'They say that the bees need to eat ten kilos of honey to make the cellules. *Imaginez-vous!*'

Madame asked what refreshment they could offer. We said we'd just had lunch; but this wouldn't satisfy Provençal hospitality. 'Just the time then for a liqueur,' she said and Monsieur fetched glasses and the tall bottle of Frigolet – the liqueur about which Daudet wove his story of L'Elixir du Père Gaucher.

'This is as full of the flowers of the Montagnette as our honey is of the flowers of the Alpilles,' remarked the old man, holding his glass of golden liquid up to the light. Then he went on to recall how he'd made his First Communion all those years ago in the Abbey on the hill. He was delighted when I told him I used to live in a house nearby.

'You know,' suddenly commented the old lady, 'you speak French better than I do.'

Although this was far from true, I knew what she meant. Left on their own, these two, like the rest of their generation, would normally speak Provençal. In our village, too, all the people of about sixty or more naturally speak Provençal; those between forty and sixty use a mixture of that and French;

but while many under forty may understand Provençal, they do not usually speak it at all. The small children also understand, because of having grandparents to baby-sit, but as soon as school age is reached all is forgotten. In some parts of Provence the language is taught once a week but in most schools not at all.

'The language is dying, as apiculture will die,' the old man said sadly. 'What with the building and the insecticides, how can bees survive?'

I asked if he agreed with the view that bees are intelligent.

'Well,' he answered, 'there are people who claim that their bees know them, but a bee only lives six months – except the queen, who goes on for three years. And she has all those eggs to lay – ten thousand at a time, they say. *Figurez-vous!* But the way they live, that's intelligent. Every bee has its job and I've seen a hive empty when a scout has come in to lead them to a newly flowering tree. Nature is wonderful – especially bees.'

The door opened and their grandson entered. Just as Daudet's couple were visited by the children from the orphanage at Eyguières, so these grand-parents too are called on and helped twice every day. We got up to go, promising to return. They raised their glasses in that great toast used by the people here when the stranger has been accepted: '*A l'amitié,*' they said.

12   To Corsica with Daudet

Having inadvertently found the old couple who so brought Daudet's story of Eyguières to life, we next followed his steps to Corsica. The three most melancholy *Lettres de Mon Moulin* are all connected with Corsica and the sea, and we were pondering over that while waiting on board the boat in Marseille harbour to sail to Ajaccio.

Sense of humour was however suddenly restored by hearing the usual announcement over the loud-speaker for visitors to leave the vessel prior to its departure. The English version ran: 'People who do not cross the sea are pleased to leave the ship.' A rendering which Daudet would certainly have appreciated.

We were in fact quite pleased to leave the ship at Ajaccio and didn't cross the sea any further to the Île des Sanguinaires. Instead we installed ourselves comfortably on the terrace of a restaurant looking across to the famous lighthouse; and to mark the occasion I ate my first sea-urchins. First and very probably last: a bottle of iodine would taste similar and be cheaper.

To reach Porto Vecchio, where originated that ship L'Emilie in which Daudet sailed with the customs men, we followed the narrow mountain roads across the centre of the island. Up and down, and round and round, and stop for the cows, and mind the pigs, and watch out for the donkeys – until we reached Zonza, a straggling village perched high on a hillside and adjacent to the most beautiful forest in Corsica.

There were two cafés in the main street but as one was too obviously modern, we went to the other, where an old, toothless lady enveloped in a black shawl seemed completely astonished by our choice. Nevertheless she smilingly beckoned us in, straight past the empty main bar with its scrupulously scrubbed wooden floor, to a little parlour behind where a huge log fire was burning in the hearth.

When we asked for coffee, she nodded, but when we further inquired if there was also something to eat and suggested bread and cheese, she flung up her hands in dismay at so much French and hurried out to call her husband. The minute he arrived, he explained with direct honesty that the coffee hadn't been made freshly that morning because they'd been working to bring in the wood for winter. Then, when we'd said we'd gladly accept the warmed up remains of yesterday's coffee, he crossed to the simple kitchen and after some searching found a pan which he set to heat on the cooker below a large Crucifix.

Still unable to believe that reheated coffee was really all we wanted to drink, he next brought a large carafe of rough, red wine. A home-made loaf and local cheese on a plate together with one jack-knife between us completed the table. To complete the picture the little old lady sat smiling and making little sounds of encouragement while rocking herself in the chair by the fire, which she coaxed continually with an ancient pair of bellows.

More than bellows were blowing when we

reached Bonifacio, which greeted us with the type of storm in which the Sémillante perished. Fortunately there were no shipwrecks that day but we did see two cars fall through holes caused by the torrential rain. Feeling safer on foot, we paddled through flooded cobblestone alleys while following one sign after another marked: The House of Napoléon. Always these notices showed an arrow pointing further and never did we arrive. Moreover all side roads seemed to lead back to the original point of departure. By dint of returning there three times we eventually interested a dog who thereafter accompanied us as far as the ramparts, from where at least there was an excellent view across to the bay described in *L'Agonie de la Sémillante*.

It was the chestnut season, for us as for Daudet. You'll remember that when the sick mariner was landed at the coast-guard's house, the family's meal was chestnuts and 'bruci', the delicious sheep's cheese of the island.

A friend from Bastia offered to take us up to her mountain village of Poggia, where one of the many chestnut forests grows. The autumnal colours were captivating: brown bracken, yellow-tinged chestnut leaves, tiny pink cyclamen and the myriad orange berries of the Arbusier bushes. The grey, bastion-type houses of the villages contrasted with the white villa-like tombs – which Daudet first remarked outside Ajaccio.

Everyone waved as we passed, even the lorry driver who had twice to move his vehicle to let us pass.

'Salut,' called the man riding one donkey and hitting another with a stick.

We couldn't help remonstrating politely.

'It needs killing before it moves,' he replied unabashed.

The chestnut harvest was in full swing; old women with sticks working alongside young lads with the sacks to be carried to the *'Fugone'*. Each country house has this special oven where the nuts are dried before being ground for flour or animal fodder.

We filled our plastic bags and later put them happily in the hotel wardrobe. But next morning . . . oh là là! The floor was covered with 'asticots', which resemble anaemic woodlice and which had gnawed their way indiscriminately through nut and bag alike.

Every day thereafter it was a case of Hunt the Asticots before the chambermaid arrived. However they came in useful one wet day when we organized asticot races! Finally on our return to Provence we astonished a farmer who found us crouched over colandered bags by a ditch, as we sorted the last reminders of a far from melancholy sojourn in Daudet's Corsica.

13   Hospital Interlude

'Eat that, Grandma. It'll do you good.'

These words, shrilly shouted and thrice repeated, gradually percolated my consciousness. I remembered then about the car accident the night before and that I'd been taken to hospital in a small Provençal town.

It was still quite early in the morning but visitors were allowed at any time of the day – some even arrived at 6.30 a.m. They just swept in with the same airy, *'Bonjour, Messieurs, Dames,'* that is said on entering a shop or bar. There was no attempt to control numbers, nor who came, nor how long they stayed, nor on children, nor what they brought.

The result was bedlam; whole families encamped for hours in the wards and baskets opened for a good feast by all who felt like eating. Meantime the usual heated arguments of the Midi arose with everyone talking at once and trying to shout each other down, while children played among the beds and in the corridors.

Altogether it was a very communal affair, a continuation of life in the small town outside. Before I could even open my eyes, I had collected quite a group of observers round the bed discussing my appearance.

'Makes you scared ever to enter a car again,' said one woman with dramatic relish.

Small town mentality also showed in the continuous exchange of news about patients. From ward to ward the latest titbits were repeated and commented upon with the same speedy enthusiasm with which information travels from street to street. Discretion is not a mark of the Midi, so that even 'So-and-So has done pipi in the bed,' was shouted happily down the line of communications.

One needed to have lived in the south to realize that the background of noise was entirely normal. Nurses slammed doors as a matter of course and when the Mistral blew the shutters crashed to and fro unchecked.

'Ca m'enerve,' a Sister screamed one particularly

windy day. But it didn't seem to have entered her head that it could also *'enerve'* the patients.

Furthermore it was considered quite normal to have transistors blaring pop music all day, and often until one o'clock at night. But the real circus was caused by four young men also recovering from a car accident. When I arrived they could not only walk about but were able to entertain the junior nurses, and when the local fête took place, they all went off to see the fireworks.

In fact it is customary here to allow patients passes to go out for the day or weekend when they are beginning to get better. Things move no faster in the hospitals of the Midi than they do in normal life, so that people expect to stay for long periods.

But to me it seemed rather like the survival of the fittest, especially as five days after my entrance my hands and feet were still as black as the moment I was picked up off the road. Mind you, the hospital was built in the time of Louis XIV and I suppose one didn't wash much in those days. A new building has long been under construction but was halted for lack of funds.

At the end of my first week a doctor demanded why I wasn't taking my pills.

'What pills?' I asked. As I couldn't turn my head, I had no idea that a daily ration of medicines had been piling up beside me – and nobody had thought to say.

One young assistant was delighted because she had been accepted for training by a London hospital. I tried to warn her without causing disillusionment but she didn't understand veiled hints and wanted concrete examples.

'Well, the bed, for instance,' I said, indicating a

mess of sheets which had been forgotten that morning and consequently not touched for thirty-six
hours. 'When the doctors come round, the patient is
expected to be looking tidy.'

But how could she be expected to see any point in
that when the only doctors she knew were as likely to
be sitting on the bed eating biscuits, and some
specialists even smoked during their visits?

Pressed for further details, I explained that it's
not usual for nurses to give their views, humorous
or otherwise, unless asked; that it would be
regarded as irregular should she be found leaning
out of a window shouting to a friend below while the
patients incidentally lie in a draught; and that ther-
mometers are not normally left for an hour, or for
the patients themselves to remove in desperation.

Above all, she was amazed that people in English
hospitals are consulted about their preference for
food. There, it was either nothing or all; take it or
leave it. Forbidden to eat for the first three days, I
was presented on the fourth with a full-blown meal,
all tinned stuff and all dumped together on a tray
such as those used in aircraft.

Upon inquiry, it appeared that, despite paying a
huge sum a day, I could not have a boiled egg unless
somebody brought it in from outside. If it hadn't
been for Fernand's arrival, I think I should have
suffered slow starvation. I understood then why
visitors arrived so well stocked and also the reason
for those first memorable words, 'Eat that, Grandma. It'll do you good.'

14. Christmas in Provence

It was a shame you couldn't be here for Christmas, as we did everything in traditional style – even the thirteen desserts. Yes, I know it sounds horrifying but in fact they mostly consist of nuts and fruit and nougat. The main exception is of a curious bun-type consistency, called *Fougasse* or *Pompe a l'Huile*, which, luckily for me, can nowadays be bought at the baker's.

Although these sweetmeats are also served after the main meal on Christmas Day, they make their first appearance on Christmas Eve. The supper then must be of fish and the thirteen desserts follow, partly to wile away the long evening until it is time to leave for Midnight Mass but, more importantly, to represent Christ and the Apostles. The thirteen dishes are set on a table covered with three cloths and lit by three candles; both in honour of the Holy Trinity.

The pride of every Provençal household is its Crib. Ours was only a tiny affair but some take up a complete corner of the living-room. Illuminated for the first time on Christmas Eve, they are filled with the world-famed Santons. In addition to the central figures of the Holy Family, the shepherds and, later, the Kings, these statuettes represent the ordinary people of Provence about their tasks of everyday life. Thus there is the gatherer of herbs, the woman collecting sticks, the girls dressed in Arlesienne costume, the knife-sharpener, the Gardians and so on.

Besides remembering to replenish the family stock of Santons before Christmas, one must also bear in mind to sow the Wheat of Sainte Barbe on December 4th. Why Sainte Barbe, Patron Saint of the Fire Brigades due to an apparent influence over lightning, should be connected with wheat sowing is still to me a mystery. The most logical answer I have so far received to my inquiries was that someone had long ago discovered that wheat sown on that day would be at exactly the right height to be cut by December 24th.

However that may be, on December 4th a handful of corn, or occasionally lentils, is placed in a large dish of watered cotton-wool and watched over zealously – for a good growth is said to denote good fortune the following year. Good or bad, the 'crop' is offered to the Child Jesus and placed in the Crib on Christmas Eve.

With our big open chimney in the Mas we are well off for burning our own yule logs and nowadays there are few public ones left to see. The custom of collecting and burning a public yule-log, called *Lou Cacha Fio*, was formerly widespread in Provence but now Martigues is one of the few centres where this is still practised.

On the Sunday prior to Christmas, a large log of olive is sprinkled with local wine before being burnt on the quay-side – while girls in traditional costume dance the Farandole around the flames. The Midnight Mass at Martigues is also made picturesque by the presence not only of this local folk-lore group but also of the fishermen, who arrive by boat along the Canal Saint Sebastien to offer fish in the church of the Madeleine.

Another port where fishermen play a particular rôle in the Christmas Mass and festivities is Palavas, towards Montpellier in Languedoc; while Les Saintes-Maries-de-la-Mer sees fishermen and gypsies intermingled. At Albaron, in the heart of the Camargue, it is a young bull which is brought by the Gardians to be blessed, but for the most part the traditional Midnight Mass of the villages incorporates an offering of a lamb by the shepherds of the region. Sometimes, as at Les Baux in the Alpilles, the lamb is pulled in a tiny cart by a ram; sometimes, as at the Abbey of Saint Michel de Frigolet in the Montagnette, to which we go so often, it is also carried in the arms of a shepherd.

These are two of the most famous and frequented centres but there are many less known places where traditional ceremonies are observed at Christmas. Good examples are St. Rémy, Barbentane (also quite near to us), Raphèle and Fontvieille, where the folkloric procession accompanied by the tambours · and fifres winds its way down the road from Daudet's Mill to the village church.

We went to 'Draw the Kings' with the cousins in Arles. Throughout January there is a long series of reunions both of families and local societies. A large *'Gâteau des Rois'* is cut into as many pieces as there are people present. One person (for our gathering it was the little boy) with his back to the cake, calls out the names, and the slices are served accordingly. Hidden in one of them is a dried bean, which makes the recipient King for the day. He is crowned with a paper crown and can, in the case of a society meeting, rule the events of the day.

That is the tradition but nowadays it is quite usual to have three plastic beans, or even figurines, in the cakes and some include a Queen. This is in fact what happened to me but fortunately with only the family present I didn't have any 'duties'.

Originally of course this get-together was only held on the Feast of the Epiphany but, as this is no longer a public holiday, the ceremony is held whenever convenient. It may even take place on New Year's Day, or during the 'Réveillons de Saint Sylvestre' on the night of December 31st. Meanwhile, in the early hours of January 1st some local bands, or 'Harmonies', for instance at Tarascon, play the 'Aubade' in the streets.

Whenever and wherever the New Year gatherings take place, you will almost certainly hear repeated the prayer first said in Provençal homes at the family reunions on Christmas Eve:

'Alegre! Alegre! Que Noste-Segne nous Alegre! S'un autre an sian pas mai, moun Dìeu, fuguen pas mens!'

'Joy! Joy! Rejoice in our Saviour! If in another year we are not more, my God, make our numbers not less!'

But next year you really must come and experience all this for yourself.

15. *Pastrage*

No, not all the Shepherds' Feasts of Provence are held on Christmas Eve. At St. Martin de Crau, for example, the 'Pastrage' takes place towards the end of January and in fact last Sunday saw us driving across the Plain of the Crau to join in the celebrations.

The Crau was once entirely barren land covered with large round stones. If you saw the Frenandel film *'Heureux qui comme Ulysse'*, you might imagine that it is still so, but like all the rest of Provençal scenery much is nowadays changed.

According to ancient legend, these stones were sent by Jupiter to aid Hercules when he ran out of arrows to shoot at the Ligurians. According to geologists, the River Durance deposited the stones there before changing to its present course. What fascinates me is a minor detail: who in the past bothered to trail all the way from here to the Crau to fetch the stones which line our flower borders?

The long-established Canal de Craponne was formerly the only water supply in an otherwise desolate area. To aid irrigation, it has recently been joined by a new canal which carries water above the plain and runs like an elongated fire-escape over the valley.

One of the resultant crops is the hay of the Crau which is the only French hay to have an official label. After it has been cut three times, the final crop is sold on the spot to the sheep-breeders of the region.

We had just reached the Pont de l'Estret, which in Provençal means a narrow bridge, and which crosses the Canal de Craponne, when the road became blocked by hundreds of sheep accompanied by two shepherds. However, it turned out that they were not on their way to the Pastrage but just following their daily routine, while being represented at the ceremony by some of their fellow shepherds.

The rendezvous was at a quarter past ten outside the Mairie of St. Martin de Crau but a good half hour beforehand a sizeable crowd had already gathered. The *boulangerie/pâtisserie* was doing a roaring trade to the girls dressed in Arlesienne or Mirielle style, to the players of tambours and fifres, to a few Gardians from the Camargue and the several young lads aspiring to be Gardians and mounted on horses of various types, colour and thickness.

Then the shepherds arrived in their long brown cloaks.

'Attention!' cried one of them standing by the steps of a cattle truck. 'We're going to let loose the escabot.'

As this is the Provençal for 'flock' all the bystanders drew back rapidly but when the ramp was lowered a solitary large ram made a royal descent.

'He's a fat one,' called one of the Gardians.

'He's eaten the hay of the Crau and not the grass of the Camargue,' bandied the shepherd.

After the ram, be-ribboned with red and green bows, had been harnessed to the tiny, white-garlanded charrette, and a lamb, looking rather bewildered but entirely resigned, had been placed inside, the procession formed.

'Allez – tambourinaires en avant et les Arlesiennes derrière,' called the M.C. Final morsels of bun were hastily swallowed. The leader of the band played a run on his fifre, or galoubet, and tapped his tambour importantly. Hiatus. *Qu'est ce qu'il se passe?* A car swirled up and a man leaped out with a bunch of staves for the shepherds.

Just in time. The M.C. gave the signal for departure, riders mounted, the girls held out their dresses gracefully, and a former shepherd took his place clutching one of the outsize red umbrellas which used to be current, and the parade began. Down the street we all followed to the forecourt of the church, where the ranks divided into lines of honour surrounding the charrette as the Curé stood on the steps to bless the gathering.

A slow march by the drums and fifres signalled the entrance into, and procession round, the church. With the Arlesiennes and Gardians in front pews and the shepherds in the sanctuary, the Mass proceeded. It was accompanied by the band and a folk-lore group sang canticles in Provençal – interrupted from time to time by the ram's deep-toned bell.

Although the sermon was in Provençal, the

Canon from Arles spoke slowly and clearly, so that it
was easy to understand how he connected the
shepherds of Bethlehem with those of Provence
today. He is one of the older preachers who are in
great demand for these local festivities, as by no
means all parish priests – in fact relatively few nowadays – can speak Provençal.

After the Creed, there were special prayers for
the shepherds present and one of them read a
poem, which he had written himself, called 'What a
Beautiful Day'. For the Offering, fruit, vegetables,
eggs, cheese, bread and milk were carried to the
altar by the Arlesiennes, and quantities of rolls were
blessed for distribution to the congregation after
the service. All was smiles and handshakes then. It
always makes a difference to have something to take
home after such an occasion and it was generally felt
to be a 'Beautiful Day' indeed.

16.   Santons of Provence

You ask about the Santons I mentioned in the
Christmas Crib, so suppose I take you on an imaginary visit to the place where we buy ours. Of course
they are for sale in all sorts of shops throughout
Provence but it is so much more satisfactory to have
personal contact with the person who makes them.

First, then, we cross the Montagnette and head
towards the Alpilles. Among the trees about two
miles before St. Rémy along the Maillane road there

is a notice reading, 'Santons de Provence'. Here we turn to follow the rough track, or '*draio*' as it is called in Provençal, which is indicated by an arrow, and so we arrive at the old Mas where lives Monsieur the Santon Maker with his wife and young daughter.

Both Monsieur and Madame are Provençal born and bred, while Monsieur comes from the village of Eyragues, only a mile or so away from where he now has his workshop for the Santons – or '*Santouns*', meaning the Little Saints. Imagine this Maître Santonnier standing in the doorway of his workshop as we arrive – a man unusually tall for the region, with greying hair, a welcoming smile and the surrounds of his eyes crinkled by sun and concentration.

With the unhurried courtesy of the country folk of the Midi he leads us into his studio, where the shelves are populated with the small clay characters which have become part of Provençal folk lore. Boxes piled high along the wall bear an amusing array of labels, such as Baker, Hunter, Holy Virgin, Angel, Gypsy and Camel. On the opposite shelves lie the corresponding moulds for these traditional figures.

The making of such plaster moulds is the most important part of the creation of a santon, for each impression must be so carefully designed that after only a few seconds' insertion the figurines emerge perfectly marked – details of clothing and facial expressions showing clearly. Because of this importance of design, Monsieur studied at the Beaux Arts in Avignon for three years. I once asked him if his father had also made santons.

'Well, no,' he said and then added with his quick smile, 'but one might say that he was on the same tack – he was a baker.'

Although most of the factory produced santons are now made of plaster, the genuine ones are made from clay. Monsieur obtains his from Marseille, and as he deftly inserts a lump into the talced mould it is easy to see that here is an accomplished artist who has been practising his craft for the past fifteen years.

He is now making the model of a woman spinning and he closes the two sides of the mould firmly together. Even pressure with his fingers and then it is almost immediately reopened, while the surplus clay is removed from the grooved channel which surrounds the form.

'*Et voilà!*' The completed figure pops out of the mould like a rabbit from a magician's hat. With a sharp knife Monsieur tidies the details and then deletes all traces of the operation by brushing over with water.

Finally the base is stamped with the official mark of the maker's name and St. Rémy-de-Provence; and the eight centimetre high woman with her tiny distaff is placed on the shelf beside all her many counterparts for preliminary drying. During the three to four days necessary for that, the clay takes on a yellow tinge but when it is baked it becomes a dull red.

Formerly the true santon was dried in the sun but now almost every Santonnier uses an oven. Not that it can be just any oven. Our Santon-Maker is most particular about his, which he lights maybe six or seven times in a year, baking as many as two thousand santons at a time. They must never come into direct contact with the heat of 850 degrees and only olive and almond wood is used, because these are, as Monsieur explains, 'full of calories but don't make too much flame'.

And so eventually to the painting, which to my mind is unfortunate. Most Southerners like crude, strong colours, which mar the delicate features so carefully formed by the artist. However the finished santons are undeniably gay and as this Santonnier's wife and daughter both help with the painting, the little workshop becomes a real family concern. Moreover, one can always buy the unpainted figures direct from a Santonnier, and this is what we do.

I remember so well the first time we visited this Master Santon-Maker. After he had taken the trouble to show and explain everything, I chose two shepherds, one clutching his hat against the Mistral, and two women gathering brushwood. Monsieur seemed pleased but quite surprised and hastened to say, 'Please don't feel you have to buy.'

And when I remarked that with such reasonable prices he'd never become a millionaire, he smiled again and said, 'We are born to work and I am lucky that my work is also a source of pleasure.'

It's about two hundred years since the first santons were made by one Jean-Louis Laguel of Marseille and nowadays, at the beginning of December, Marseille has its annual Santon Fair. Wander among the booths as you will, but if it's the traditional spirit of the Christmas Crêche and the genuine hand-made santon of clay that you seek, come also with us at any time of the year to visit our Maître Santonnier on the Maillane road outside St. Rémy-de-Provence.

17. Markets and Herbs

I don't know why you should imagine that our living here constitutes a shopping problem. On the contrary we are better served than many people nearer town, for twice a week a travelling shop calls at each Mas in the area. Both vans are excellently stocked with everything from brushes to butter, and as the Thursday van comes from one village and the Saturday one from another, prices are kept interesting. Our only real needs from the shops are bread and stamps; or a wider selection of meat than is transported around.

In fact, however, so long as we have the car, we like to 'Do' the markets as well. Sometimes there are really worth-while bargains and always there is plenty of interest.

Our local market is on the tiny scale of the village but one can nonetheless buy, for example, shoes and household goods. Arles has the biggest markets of the region, bi-weekly, but it is rather far for us to visit often. Nevertheless we've recently bought such diverse articles as watch straps and a bath mat from the stalls on the Lices. From Tarascon, which is a sizeable market, some of our latest acquisitions include four goldfish, two dresses and a straw hat – the dimensions of its brim being recommended for 'Working among the vegetables but not for picking apricots.' The autumnal Tarascon Fair, which, as well as having amusements to offer, attracts an extra number of street traders, is another profitable occasion to do shopping.

A particularly picturesque market is the Wednesday one at St. Rémy as, apart from all the usual booths, there are usually several colourful flower stalls, displaying plants from the local growers of horticultural seeds. Frequently, too, there is a long stall of attractively packeted herbs, presided over by a stocky, cheerful, grey-haired woman in a check apron.

I've always been surprised that she considered it worth while setting up such a display, since most of us who live in Provence have only to go out and pick the herbs we want for ourselves. So the other day I asked her how she managed to make a living. She gave me a knowing wink and tapped the side of her nose in the conspiratorial gesture used by the people here when conveying special information.

'It's the tourists, God bless them! One only has to see a group of tourists coming and, *op là! c'y est!*' She rubbed her hands together expressively. 'Our usual ground is by the Pont du Gard. You understand, hein?'

We inquired if she knew all the uses of the herbs. She winked again and beckoned us behind the stall, where a printed list of herbs and their uses was hanging for quick reference.

Did she collect the herbs herself?

'*Moi? Pardi!*' She was the merchant; she only packeted the herbs.

Shortly afterwards we met the two local herboristes, who live in a charming little house near the centre of the village. They laughed when the stall was mentioned.

Monsieur, a round-faced, ruddy-cheeked man, said with a broad smile, 'We work with our hands, others with the *sous*. It's we who have the hard work.'

He and Madame and their son are all collectors of herbs. They range far and wide to find the plants required for medicinal and culinary uses. It is a bi-seasonal occupation – spring and autumn – for if the plants are picked in summer flower, the leaves fall when dried.

'Mind you,' remarked Monsieur, as contemptuously as his benevolent nature allowed, 'the merchants who sell to tourists will accept anything at any time.' And he went on to talk about the export trade which has grown up recently in packeted herbs. It seems that all too often the thyme, for example, is picked in Algeria, where it is an inferior variety, and a sprig or two of Provençal thyme added to give the stronger scent.

Madame then joined in the conversation and opened her cupboard to show us how dried thyme should look when collected at the proper season. As she took it from the jar, none fell. Like all country folk, she uses a great deal of thyme, rosemary and sage in her cooking. Thyme is also drunk widely as an infusion to aid digestion, sage as a tonic and rosemary for colds and flu.

I asked the herborists if they believed the old story that a distillation of rosemary and alcohol had caused an elderly queen of Hungary to rejuvenate to the extent of being asked for in marriage by the king of Poland.

Monsieur rubbed a hand over a stubbly chin and, after consideration, judged the matter unlikely. It is part of the Provençal's habitual courtesy to listen attentively to another person's words, even when they lack depth.

We went back to talk of the curative properties of infusions made from various plants. Fennel taken after a meal disperses wind in the stomach; lime-leaves or verbena act as sedatives; wild lavender is a slight anti-septic for the respiratory tract; camomile cures stomach disorders and headaches.

We wondered if among all the herbs they picked, they had particular favourites of their own.

'*Marjoram,*' answered Madame promptly. 'Crush it in boiling water and inhale the vapours for a cold.'

'*Madwort,*' stated Monsieur categorically. 'Best possible thing to calm a cough. But,' he added roguishly, 'that's one you won't find on a stall for the tourists, you know!'

18. *The Vanniers' Village*

Last night we had visitors from Vallabrègues. I can't remember whether I ever told you about this little place – for Vallabrègues is a village with a difference. The most obvious peculiarity to the outsider is that while geographically in the department of the Bouches du Rhône, it is officially in the Gard – which lies on the other side of the river.

This is because the topography changed. Vallabrègues was in fact on the other side of the river but one nineteenth century day the Rhône burst its banks and altered course, so that the villagers found themselves in alien land. For, as maybe I've mentioned, the Gard originally formed part of Languedoc and France, whereas what is now the Bouches du Rhône always belonged to the Realm of Provence.

In this way Vallabrègues lived up to its name, which signifies 'Lips of the Stream', and today it continues to do so equally dramatically, for it is at Vallabrègues that the big new dam has recently been constructed across the Rhône. Now one can stand above the water and watch the 'lips of the stream' dividing down in a rush of miniature Niagara.

It is also largely due to the river that the place owes its other outstanding interest, because its banks were formerly thicketed with long lines of willows and thus Vallabrègues became the village of the vanniers, or basket weavers. The character of Vincent in *Mireille* was a vannier from Vallabrègues and this brings many literary minded tourists to see the weavers at work.

Not that it is especially easy to find them. I well remember the first time an English friend and I arrived there one hot, still summer afternoon. The village slept but the proprietor of the café in the main square stirred himself to give us directions. Nevertheless it wasn't long before we lost ourselves in the labyrinths of small streets. Not a soul in sight. Not even a sound in the heat.

'We'd better come back in the evening when there's someone about,' said my friend.

'You may be quite sure that not only are there people about,' I replied, 'but also that they are watching us right now. A strange car in a village never passes unnoticed.'

And sure enough we just then caught sight of a hand moving a curtain gently aside. A few seconds more and man's head appeared at the window.

'Who are you looking for?'

We explained and were told to turn through a gateway and knock at a door marked 'Bureau'. No reply. We called, 'Ho!' as one calls in Provence and an amiable dog appeared, looked at us, started back the way he'd come and then stopped and looked again. As it seemed obvious he thought we should follow, we did; past troughfuls of soaking canes and into a large workshop where four men were sitting on boards on the floor.

Certainly we were more surprised than they: the Provençal is not easily surprised.

'Don't you find it hard?' I asked, astonished by the uncomfortable looking position.

'Pardi!' one weaver replied. 'But the behind gets used to it, you know. It's been sitting here every day for the past thirty years.'

The owner then took us to the display room. Floor to ceiling was stocked with baskets of all types, made in cane either from the Tarn area or Spain – for there are no local willows left and the reeds of the Camargue are now rarely used in the weaving.

The greatest disaster to our eyes was the bright varnishing with which most of the articles were finished. Monsieur le Patron shrugged.

'Qu'est ce que vous voulez?' he said. 'My biggest market nowadays is to the tourists at Les Baux, and this is what they like.'

But another well known vannier of Vallabrègue compromises with modernity. He advertises bucket-shaped baskets called after Brigitte Bardot but keeps most of his wares in natural cane. The sixty-six articles in his catalogue are sold as far afield as Japan but Monsieur recognizes philosophically that the art of vannerie is dying.

'Both my father and my grandfather were basket-weavers,' he said the other day, as Fernand and I stood in his workshop which has the traditional vannier's tools hung on its walls. 'Once, every family in the village had at least one member a vannier and people in the region naturally expected their baskets to come from Vallabrègues. Farmers used cane skips to carry the fruit to market; chemists wrapped their medicine bottles in woven reed. But with the synthetic materials all that is finished. There are no young vanniers here today, so the art must die out.'

Monsieur stopped to push his beret back as he surveyed the pile of goods which may take from one hour to one day to finish.

'This is the work of four craftsmen,' he sighed. 'Imagine what the output was like when there were a hundred! And when these men reach retirement age in a few years' time, the doors of this workshop will close on an era.'

A melancholy thought, but the Provençal is never melancholy for long and Monsieur wrapped his foulard round his neck to cross the courtyard to his house in search of apéritifs for us all. While we drank them he spoke of his days as musician in the local band and we were soon all cheered.

Personally I think some basket-weaving will always continue in the village but even without it Vallabrègues will now remain noteworthy – for with its giant dam once more changing the course of the Rhône, the 'Lips of the Stream' will be marked on the map for ever.

19. Van Gogh in Provence

I'm sorry but I don't agree with your artist friend. If
as she says Van Gogh was just a 'Lugubrious, miser-
able man with a twisted mind who spent an unfortunate and tormented period exiled in Provence
towards the end of his life,' he could never have
written from Arles to his brother Theo, 'I am so
happy in the house and in my work.' And in another
letter a short time later, 'I love Provence unreservedly.'

Of course he had his problems and set-backs;
everybody suffers from them wherever they live.
His pecuniary embarrassments began long before
he moved south. He had, too, the special trials which
all of us who live in Provence share – the Mistral
above all, the dust, the sometimes merciless sun,
the natural inquisitiveness of some of the neighbours. But all these things are incidentals and in
no way alter a deep affection for the region and
its people.

It was only February in 1888 when he first came
south and among his earliest recorded impressions
are those of the snow, which was two feet deep on his
arrival. Immediately he observed the Japanese print
effects, which arose from the snow and from the
colours and shapes of rocks and cypress in the clear
light of the Midi.

It was this light and the rapidly changing tones

which made him work so fast. He realized that people might call him slapdash but felt that the only hope of reproducing what he saw with any faithfulness lay in speed of approach.

Perhaps your friend needs to live in Provence before she can understand this attitude. Crops ripen, flowers bloom, grass browns with such rapidity that the scenery is never static; while just to watch the reflection of a sunset on the Alpilles is to witness an infinity of indescribable hues. Changes of weather, too, often have dramatic outcome in the Midi. Sharp silhouettes of a morning may be rounded softness by afternoon. So it's not surprising that Van Gogh was fascinated by the mutations of orchards, cornfields, vineyards and olive groves; or that he found it necessary to recommence his picture of the Langlois drawbridge because of altered conditions.

Visitors to Arles today who are aware that this bridge was demolished, may be surprised to see a sign-post showing showing three kilometres to 'Van Gogh's Bridge'. An identical drawbridge some forty kilometres away has been dismantled and re-erected on the site of the one that was destroyed.

The Trinquetaille bridge, on the other hand, is now entirely different; the 'little yellow house', where Gauguin joined the Dutchman, has disappeared and the bar where he originally had rooms has been rebuilt. No all-night cafés exist today in Arles: the site of the one haunted by the painters is covered by a furniture store.

This is not to say that the Arles which Van Gogh knew and loved is no longer to be found. One has only, for example, to wander through the narrow streets and stand beside the old church of St. Mary

Major looking across to the distant Crau plain, to recapture the ambiance familiar to him.

From the same viewpoint can be seen the ruined Abbey of Montmajour, which he visited about fifty times – occasionally in the company of the Zoave lieutenant whose portrait he painted – while nearby is the arena where he went to some of the bull fights. Afterwards he described them objectively, making no mention of any emotions aroused in himself.

The Millet-type scenes of peasants which he noted near Fontvielle can still be seen in many a Provençal field, though Fontvielle itself has been regrettably ruined by the flow of tourists to Les Baux and the so-called Mill of Daudet. This was anticipated by Van Gogh, for he commented that outsiders with money were already spoiling the district, and added cynically and prophetically that probably some of them would soon be painting sheep-filled landscapes for boxes of chocolates.

He revelled in Daudet's books about the legendary Tartarin and went several times to Tarascon. He painted on the road between there and Arles and did a picture of the diligence in the inn. It was, in fact, after a visit to Tarascon that he wrote the sentence, 'I love Provence unreservedly'. Happily it is a place which remains almost unspoilt today – a good example of a true Provençal town.

Quite the opposite must be said of Les-Saintes Maries, which then was only a tiny fishing centre and is now a paradise for trippers – albeit on the far shore there still lie boats such as those which attracted the artist's eye. He sketched them very early in the morning before they put out to sea – the Mediterranean which made this northerner exclaim, 'Now that I have seen the sea here, I am absolutely convinced of the importance of staying in the Midi.'

Back in Arles, the outside at least of the hospital remains the same (although a new one has recently been built). This was the general hospital to which he was taken after the unfortunate incident of cutting his ear. Incoming patients today also enter through the archway into the courtyard with white arcades and pass the plaque commemorating its foundation in the sixteenth century by Charles IX.

In this oasis of quiet, it is easy to picture the postman, Roulin, on his way in to visit his artist friend. By spring 1889, however, Roulin had left for Marseille and Vincent agreed to go to the home for mentally disturbed people run by the nuns at St.

Paul de Mausole, outside St. Rémy. Almost immediately he wrote to his brother remarking how glad he was to have done so. 'I have never been so peaceful as here and in the hospital in Arles.'

Although Van Gogh admitted that his picture of the Reaper here represented Death, he wrote of it, 'There is nothing sad in this death, it goes its way in broad daylight with a sun flooding everything with a light of pure gold!'

People also often try to connect the gnarled olives with a twisted mind but the painter said of them, 'I tried to express the time of day when you see the green rose beetles and the cicadas flying about in the heat. . . . I sought contrasting effects in the foliage, changing with the hues of the sky.'

New olives have now been planted in the same field outside the walls of St. Paul. In a field on the other side it is easy to find the spot where his easel stood as he painted the hills above the site of ancient Glanum. For myself, I like best to sit by the great stones of the former quarry, whose shades of green and ochre he found so satisfactory.

Towards the end of his stay in St. Rémy, Van Gogh began to find the religious atmosphere oppressive but he must still have appreciated the most charming romanesque cloisters in Provence beside the small monastery church, where outsiders still intermingle with patients for the Sunday Mass.

Happily there is no attempt at commercialism. Not only is there no collection taken at the Mass but there is no charge for entering either the cloisters or the museum, which shows the type of accommodation Van Gogh had and is decorated with reproductions of his paintings. Here, too, hang Theo's letter requesting admission for his thirty-six year old brother as a third class boarder, and a page from the register showing that he entered as a voluntary patient.

He could have returned to the north but stayed here voluntarily in order to continue with the work which was flowing from him in response to these surroundings. He rose to the challenge of the light, colours and shapes by trying out new techniques which he enthusiastically described in detail to Theo. In Provence he felt there was everything needed 'to do good work' and here it was that his artistry flowered. Scarcely a period of 'Unfortunate and tormented exile.'

20. Tales Past and Present

In this land where instead of inquiring which road to take to a new address the people ask, 'Who are the neighbours?' there is an inevitable fund of good tales to be told.

Unfortunately television is gradually killing the former exchange of visits which took place, especially in winter, from Mas to Mas. All the people from around who have come to call since we've been established here remark, 'I remember this Mas so well from the days when we used to get together for an evening of cards, or at the chestnut season, or to make "Oreillettes" (a hard type of sweet fritter, often orange flavoured)– those were the days to hear the best stories.'

Nevertheless it still holds good that whenever a group of Provençals is gathered the tales continue to be told and recollections aired. Moreover, as the country folk in particular have long memories, a story-telling session will often begin with episodes from their grandparents' time. Just so the other day, a woman recounted as if it had happened yesterday:

'Grandma was putting us children to bed. We lived on the first floor and the goat lived underneath. Suddenly there were footsteps on the stairs and we were afraid. "If you don't go away . . ." began my grandmother – but she couldn't think of a threat to finish with. So as the steps came on upwards she opened the door and flung our chamber pot at the intruder. But it was the goat, you see. He'd heard voices and come upstairs to investigate. Well, he had more fright than my grandmother and ran off with the pot stuck on his horns.'

Another woman took up the grandparent thread:

'It was about fifty years ago. My grandfather decided to go to the village feast. He called to his daughters to bring his coat and they laid it on his bed. At the last minute, however, he left it behind and after he'd gone it slipped onto the floor.

'When one of his daughters came back to the room, she found the coat in a hump as if someone were underneath. She screamed so loudly that the neighbours came running and stood around the supposedly concealed robber. One man had his gun and cried, "If you move, I fire. If you don't come out, I fire." Nothing moved and at last someone plucked up courage to jump on top of the marauder. And of course the coat collapsed, as there was nothing there.'

Everyone laughed and I said, 'All the same, it's

good to think that they all came running to help.'

'Yes,' said one of the younger men present, 'but in Provence we still do help each other over difficulties. Did you hear about the worker who sat by the Durance during the événements in May 1968?'

And when I told him I hadn't, he resumed:

'He was a small, hen-pecked man with a large wife who didn't agree with strikes. As he simply didn't dare to tell her that the factory where he worked was closed, he took his sandwiches as usual each morning and went to sit by the Durance all day. His workmates were so sorry for the poor little man that they clubbed together from the small funds they had to give him the money to take home on the usual pay-day.'

Policemen and priests are always popular subjects for tales of every generation. Perhaps the best episode concerning the disliked traffic police, or 'flics', was the one said to have happened on the crowded N.7 during the first summer that the breathalyser was introduced.

The story goes that they stopped a man whose driving was wavering and presented him with the bag. But he fumbled about and blew wrongly, so one of the flics said, 'Not like that, you old fool, like this.' And he blew hard into the breathalyser. Green were its contents and red was his face, as the patrol car rapidly drove away.

As for priests, the current story concerning one village curé is at least substantially true – although there were no witnesses to the vital scene.

The Sacristan there came of shepherd stock and was extremely proud of his position of responsibility in the church. He bowed people into the pews, restored lost belongings to their owners, served the

Mass in stately fashion and took round the collection bag most ceremoniously. Meantime he became a man of small means and bought a property across the fields.

In the sacristy stood two valuable candlesticks and, alas, one feast day Monsieur the Sacristan and Monsieur the Curé disputed as to whether these precious objects should or should not be displayed. So the curé was left with his candlesticks and the sacristan left his church and is now to be seen with a newly acquired flock of sheep. The other shepherds will tell you the tale with respect – an ex-sacristan shepherd is someone to be reckoned with, after all.

On the other hand, the country curé himself has often an excellent fund of stories. Our Mas was blessed by the priest who had married us – a good Marseillais talking a racy language, spiced by belly-laughs and enlivened still further by the telling attitudes and gestures used by the true raconteur of the Midi.

After the short ceremony, as we were gathered round the table with our neighbours, he took a pinch of snuff, leaned forwards and remarked that he'd recently been helping the curé of Eyragues with the annual Solemn Communions. Since we are all aware that this was no casual observation but would surely lead to the latest story, we waited.

'You know what they say about Eyragues?' he asked, raising his eyebrows at each of us in turn. We didn't.

'It's just what they say, of course,' he underlined with a slightly malicious quirk of the lips, 'but they say that the people there are famed for sleight of hand. Leave something lying about one moment, and, whoosh, the next it's gone.

'Well, this year, as you know, the crops are behind and the annual three-day fête at Eyragues coincides with the time for planting the peas. Now a certain elderly peasant particularly enjoyed the festivities and despite the pressure of work abandoned the Mas for the village. The first day his wife said nothing. The second day she complained. The third she insisted forcibly that at least he should drill the lines so that she could sow the peas.

'I drilled them yesterday evening,' answered the old man, preparing to leave once more for the festivities.

'But his wife determined that first they should both go to the field in question. Needless to say, not a line had been prepared and the good woman turned on her man in righteous anger. As quick as a flash her husband flung up his arms in surprised indignation.

'Sapristi!' he cried. 'They've gone from where I traced them. Somebody must have pinched them in the night.'

Of course to relish the full savour of such a tale you need not only to see the speaker but also to hear it in the original Provençal. It's a language much easier to understand than to speak. So hurry up and come and enjoy for yourself such stories as they are told.

21. The Linking People

Since I finished my last letter with a slightly scandalous story of Eyragues, I'll begin this one by saying that, as an outsider unconcerned with local reputations, I have always particularly liked this village. A calm oasis on the now busy route between St. Rémy and Châteaurenard, it is unnoticed by tourists, despite having a church with a fourth-century chapel.

Once every month in the market place you can see a tinker installed, in the sun in winter and in the shade in summer. Whatever the weather, he unfailingly makes a monthly journey from St. Rémy to sit here in the square and mend the old pots and pans which people equally unfailingly continue to bring. Formerly the tinker was a common sight; now he is a rarity and this is one of the few people left who link us to the Provence of the past.

Formerly, too, there were chestnut vendors all along the Lices when the autumn came to Arles. Now there is only one of them left also. Each October he pushes his brazier on a barrow to a strategic position by a corner of the Lices and here he continues the unhurried and thorough work that he has always done. For he is most particular that the nuts are done to a turn and no matter how many people are pressing around he won't be hustled.

With deft fingers he continues to fashion the

newspaper cornets; while lifting the enshrouding sack from time to time and keeping up a lively running commentary on progress beneath. No chestnuts could taste better and he knows this and is proud of his reputation.

Another well-known personage connects the now over-modern Port St. Louis with its past; and she very nearly ceased to do so last winter when she became ill. This is an elderly grandmother, who for as long as anyone in St. Louis can remember has sold fish in the streets. Not only among the un-pretentious houses of yesterday but also between the blocks of concrete flats, can the people of St. Louis still hear that high-pitched cry of the reputedly oldest fish-seller in France: *'O Pei! O Pei!'*

Tarascon, too, has its linking people. Once a week a shrill trumpeting superimposes the normal noises of traffic and roadworks. Not so very long ago the small trompette was used by many different kinds of street traders – the mender of pans, like the one in Eyragues, the sweep, the rag and bone man, the knife-sharpener, the milkman – to name just a few.

The man with the milk has entirely disappeared from the scene; there is one knife-sharpener who still occasionally sits under the arcades in the Rue des Halles; the rag and bone man passes from time to time while shouting to attract attention; and I once met a sweep and his wife walking the narrow back streets with a quaint sing-song call. All the rest have succumbed to modern methods,which prove more profitable than the leisurely and personal round of selling in the streets. All except one, for the shrill trumpet of Thursday mornings is followed by a voice raucous with wear, crying, *'Pognes'.*

Pognes are cakes of a bun-like consistency, made

with butter and shaped like coronets. They originated at a place called Romans, in the Drôme; and there are people who say that no real Pognes have existed since the day they ceased to be produced there. Be that as it may, they are now made at Aubagne, in the Bouches du Rhône, and consequently sold from door to door in such centres as Tarascon.

When, with his basket of cakes on his arm, he wends his fanfared way through streets broad and narrow, crying, *'Pognes, Pognes'*, this merchant from the past somehow resembles Molly Malone almost as strongly as does the old grandma who sells fish in St. Louis.

It was after I had put a foot through an ancient stool that we discovered the delightful little lady who still practises the craft of rush-weaving. She lives in one of the narrow streets which form the old interior of Tarascon town and her husband opened the door. Rightly proud of his wife and her work, he said at once, 'Oh yes, she could do it. Just like that, she could. But when will she have the time?'

Nevertheless she managed to squeeze our little piece in between the bigger orders and she herself brought the stool back to us, looking better than it had ever done before. I asked her for how long she had been practising the craft.

'I began work at twelve in a factory at Beaucaire,' she said. 'Eight centimes a week they paid us and twelve for each piece finished. If it wasn't well done, they came and cut it and we cried. When you think you've gained the piece, after hours of work, and then there's nothing, it's hard, you understand.

'They didn't keep us at school in those days,' she continued, 'but they didn't really teach us the craft either. We just had to watch and copy, and often we made mistakes, being so young as we were, and that's when it was cut. That's the way we learnt in those days, the hard way. But it's stood me in good stead ever since.'

We wondered what sort of work came her way today, and she replied in the same calm tone of one who has come to terms with life, 'Work comes with the people. One never knows. A gentleman from Paris arrived the other day with a chair that had the most enormous feet you ever saw.'

And we realized that so far as we were concerned we would always be connected with our little stool, because her work becomes identified with the person who brings it. Interest in individuals and pride of work, are the marks of all these people who link us so well to the past.

22.   The Gardian

No, no and no again! The so often mentioned Gardian of the Camargue is by no means just a French version of the television cowboy. Although today there is unfortunately and inevitably a certain amount of what the local people term 'cinema' for the tourists, the genuine Gardian's only similarity to the screen gallopers is his horsemanship. Confront reality with imagination and one is often surprised. To prove the point, I'll introduce you to a certain real-life Gardian.

After a first quick glance you'll almost certainly remark that he is far from being your idea of a horseman. His well-filled stomach doesn't give the impression of taking much exercise of any kind and his slightly hooded eyes convey a false suggestion of lethargy. Yet he is not only a superb horseman but one of the best known Gardians of the Camargue.

We first met two years ago in the courtyard of the Mas where he is the chief Gardian of one of the big manades of bulls, and where a large number of the white Camargue ponies are also bred. As Gérard Gadiot wrote in his book *En Camargue*, 'Here the passion for horses and the passion for bulls go hand in hand; it is a profound passion, almost a religion, a faith, *La fé di bioù*, or the belief in the bull, we say here, and to satisfy it, the Gardian will brave the elements, endure the worst fatigue and even risk his life; and all that whether he is rich or poor, young or old, cultured or ignorant. He is not just a horseman but a cavalier of the *"Countesso"*, which is an old name for Provence. . . . It is a race of men apart.'

This is certainly as good a description as any of our Gardian and his companions, twentieth-century inheritors of the traditions of the Antico Counfrarie di Gardian de Sant-Jorge, which was founded at the beginning of the sixteenth century.

One of these traditions faithfully followed during these past 500 years is the Feast of the Gardians, which takes place every year about the beginning of May. On this occasion the new captain and priors of the Confrérie are elected and the standard formally handed over; there are cavalcades round Arles and equestrian games; there is the Mass of St. George with canticles and sermon in Provençal and the Gardians afterwards distributing the specially blessed bread to the local orphanage. In addition to all this, nowadays on the same occasion the annual Queen of Arles is usually presented to the people of the town with a guard of honour by the Gardians, while Provençal dances are performed by various folklore groups.

This is the glamorous side of the life of a Gardian, which has little connection with his daily round; although certainly there is far less hardship and far less adventure in his life now than in the former days. Then the Camargue was entirely wild swamp instead of the acres of modern rice-fields and the vast areas which are now enclosed and forbidden to the public. Then he really lived in the cabane which today has become such a tourist attraction that it is even possible to hire one by the hour.

The inside of a genuine cabane is divided into kitchen and bedroom. Its rounded back stands to the cold Mistral; it is thatched with reeds above white plaster walls and crowned with a small cross. This famous cross of the Gardians, which marked the wastelands, incorporates a heart and an anchor, representing faith, hope and charity. The edges of the cross are shaped like the tridents carried by the Gardians to herd the bulls. 'A single point would not be sufficient for their tough hides,' our special Gardian once explained.

The traditional costume of the Gardian is now mostly to be seen on local feast days. The grey or beige trousers narrow below the knee to avoid wrinkling and are generally braided. Shirts are often check but may be of any colour, preferably bright. Neat velour waistcoats cover them for special occasions; while the foulard, which is frequently in the red and gold colours of Provence, can be worn either round the neck or as a belt. The wide-brimmed felt hat is a protection against the sun and bad weather alike, and neither that nor the compact spurs over the low elasticated boots have any resemblance to the flamboyant appendages of most cowboys on film.

The usual saddle has a high pommel which can take two saddle-bags and is also higher at the back, so that the Gardian sits in the dip between. This is said to be one reason why the Camargue pony is never taught to trot – the gallop being much more comfortable for the rider in this position.

'It's the rider that makes the horse,' said the Gardian that day of our first encounter, and he went on to describe the painstaking months of work which go into the training of a horse before it can be used with the bulls. The first lessons begin when the colt is about three years old and he will be at least four and a half before being passed as a finished product.

The trot was dismissed as irrelevant.

'It's not natural, that's all,' he said with the authority of one who has lived in the wild with the herds of untamed horses. 'No more is shoeing,' he added with a contemptuous snort for the men who shoe horses for use by the tourist trade.

There is a real craze now for these so-called 'ranches' where visitors jog uncomfortably on unfortunate mounts to 'see the bulls', or just 'promenade,' sometimes followed by the attraction of a *grillade au bois* or barbecue. The mock gardians who supervise these outings would perhaps be out of their depth in a conversation with this real one, who can talk at length on the natural phenomena concerned with horses. Maybe they know that the young Camargue pony is not born white, but they

are unlikely to be able to hold an audience spell-
bound, as he can, with authentic descriptions of the
fierce fights among the stallions of a herd left wild.

There is no doubt that he loves and lives for his
horses and bulls. Undeterred by severe injuries
recently received when a bull burst the barricades,
he is back again in the saddle as nonchalant as ever.
If it is the rider who makes the horse, it is certainly
the man who makes the Gardian – and, as you'll now
realize, he has no banal connection with those cowboys of television!

23.   *Course Libre*

I had a feeling that the reference to bulls in my last
letter would arouse some reaction from you! The
bull is synonymous with the Camargue and with
Provence but, on the whole, those of us who get hot
under the collar when the subject of bull-fighting is
mentioned, have no need to do so where Provence is
concerned.

I say 'on the whole', because it must unfortunately
be admitted that the *Mise à Mort,* or bull-fight
Spanish style with its culminating point of the death
of the bull, is held on the big public holidays, or
Ferias, in Arles and Nimes. These are, however, not
only in Spanish style but with Spanish matadors and
bulls transported from Spain.

The bull of the Camargue is a different sort of
beast, full of individual characteristics. He is

beloved by the people as a symbol of their region and many of the animals which are used in the ring are known by their names and spoken of as friends.

As I've already told you, where once the Camargue was entirely wild, it is now largely under cultivation, so that the places where herds of bulls may roam become progressively scarcer. It is also by no means a profitable business to breed these black, stocky creatures with their high horns.

Yet although there are fewer manades today, the tradition continues and is partly a matter of local pride and prestige. There are even still some people who have the old feeling (although rarely recognized as such) that to face a bull not only proves one's manhood but that in some vague way the courageous spirit of the animal is transmitted by the contact.

The herding and branding of young bulls is an occasion of festivity which always draws large crowds. Local clubs organize outings to the manades for these *'Ferrades'*. Sometimes a monster dish known as Aioli (a mixture of meat, often snails, and vegetables eaten with a garlic mayonnaise) is served afterwards; sometimes there's a *'Méchoui'* (a sheep roasted whole); always a good deal of liquid flows.

Another occasion when all the public gathers is the day that bulls are run through the streets of a town or village for an *'Abrivado'*, and young men are never then lacking to show their courage. This game – for game it is, even if a somewhat dangerous one – consists of a group of Gardians on their white Camargue ponies sending several bulls galloping down an advertised course, while the pedestrians endeavour to break up the bunch.

When this happens, most people take cover

mighty quickly, for it is common knowledge that whereas you can walk through a herd of bulls in a field without too much worry, it's as well not to have to face one alone. I must admit that personally I prefer to watch an Abrivado from the safety of a first-floor window!

But 'going to the bulls' in Provence generally means going to what is known as a *'Course Libre'*, or a *'Course à la Cocarde'*, where there are no horses, no swords, no capes, no picadors and no death – at least not of the bull. It is a straight-forward confrontation of man and beast. The latter has two cockades fixed behind his horns and the former manoeuvres to remove them without getting tossed or ripped on the way.

We went to a *Course Libre* in Mouries the other day. Outside the romanesque church we were stopped by a bon homme in a vivid check beret and blue jeans, who was repeating like a record the directions for the Arènes. And there were plenty of children trying to get a pre-view of the bulls already waiting in the Toril.

All seats in the shade had long since been sold and the atmosphere in the Arènes was mounting. The man hawking paper-hats did a brisk trade in creations of blue and yellow in mock gardian style. The vendors of peanuts and chocolate ices vied to shout the loudest but the crowd's attention was split between a portly amateur trumpeter and the parading *'razeteurs'* – the young men, dressed in white, who would shortly be facing the bulls.

Twenty minutes before the opening, canned music was added to the cacophony of shrilled remarks, barking dogs, crying babies – there were several in prams and two in arms – and a tape recorder relaying another bull fight to complete the ambiance. Despite all this, the man next to us slept profoundly, sprawled across the hard stone stand with his beret pulled over his face.

Then the President and Judges entered the Tribune d'Honneur. Four o'clock struck and the music appropriately changed to Carmen while the razeteurs marched into the ring. The door of the Toril slid back and the first bull galloped in, came to an abrupt halt, pawed the sawdust and charged the first white figure within sight.

Excitement tensed as cockades were snatched or narrowly missed, horns grazed clothing if not skin and one of the red and yellow barricades was broken. And so for six bulls. When the razeteurs showed some signs of tiring, additional prize money was offered by local patrons and announced over the microphone by way of encouragement.

And all the time in the crowd bets were being made on the bulls, which were discussed by name and character. I suppose it's hard to understand unless one lives in the atmosphere, so you'll just have to take my word for it when I say that the bull to the people is neither an enemy, nor just an animal, but rather a personality and in some way a personification of the spirit of Provence.

24. Provençal Cooking

So the Aioli whetted your appetite! Personally I
think it's most tasty when it does include snails, but,
whatever the meat, it is, of course, the garlic sauce
which gives it the particular savour. Garlic is often
called the Perfume of the Midi and we certainly use
it in a great number of dishes. For example, our
daily salad (and here that doesn't mean a mixture
but just lettuce or other green leaves) is covered with
a dressing made from crushed garlic, oil, vinegar,
salt and pepper.

Naturally there is garlic too in the Bouillabaisse of
Marseille, though the saffron is perhaps its main
mark. Useless to give you instructions for making
the Boui-abaisso (as it is written in Provençal, meaning Boil on a low light), as you could never find all
the necessary types of fish involved.

On the other hand, you could easily make the
equally renowned *Soupe au Pistou*, and very good it
is. As it happens, we are having it for supper
tonight, so the recipe comes direct. Dice a pound of
green beans (or here the red-podded variety are
often used) three or four potatoes and two good
sized tomatoes. Season well and boil until about
three-quarters cooked; then add some vermicelli
and simmer slowly. The people of this area frequently add other vegetables, such as courgettes,
thus making a sort of Minestrone with the Pistou

sauce finally added. The essential is that the soup is really thick – to the point of a spoon standing upright in it.

Shortly before serving, pound together three garlic cloves with the leaves from a branch of basil and four small teaspoons of oil. Wet it with a little of the soup and pour it into the tureen with a handful of grated cheese. Add the rest of the soup and stir well. Hope you like it.

Being a good Provençal, Fernand likes his soup every evening; winter and summer alike. In the same way, the main meal of the day – at mid-day – always begins with some sort of *hors d'oeuvre*. His favourite is raw celery in anchovy butter but he also likes various vegetables in *vinaigrette* sauce – not only asparagus and artichoke (raw when tender) but spinach, green beans, beetroot, lentils and so on. Olives go well with the spiced sausages of the region, especially the *Saucisson d'Arles*. Both the green and black olives of Provence are excellent but we prefer the black ones prepared with herbs by a merchant in Fontvieille.

Then, of course, the straightforward fresh tomato salad, sprinkled with parsley and/or onions, is an ever popular *hors d'oeuvre* in Provence, for the tomato is as widely used here as garlic and is the base of a great many recipes. In fact I sometimes feel that I pass a disproportionate amount of my time browning onions in oil and then adding either fresh tomatoes or the concentrated form known as *coulis*, before continuing with whatever dish is under preparation.

A rather pleasant example of this kind is *Veau Champignons*. After the onions are coloured and before adding about a tablespoonful of coulis, brown pieces of seasoned veal (floured or not, as wished). Cover with water, add salt, pepper, bay leaf and nutmeg. When boiling, tip in some dried flap mushrooms, or cèpes (previously soaked) and simmer for at least an hour and a half.

Variations on the tomato sauce theme are often served with what are loosely terms '*pâtes*'. This covers all types of macaroni, spagetti etc., and I never cease to be surprised at the vast quantities consumed. It would be interesting to know whether this dates back to the days of the Province of Rome, or whether it is merely due to the proximity of Italy. After all, Spain is as near and the only connection with Spanish cooking is the use of oil – which applies to all Mediterranean countries.

The *Tomates Provençals* served in hotels are often catastrophic, because they have been reheated too often and over-swim in oil. Made at home they are both simple and good. Cut the tomatoes across in half, empty the pulp and mix it with minced meat, bread, garlic, parsley, salt and pepper. Lightly fry the tomato cases and refill with the mixture. Cover with bread crumbs and a dab of butter and cook in a slow oven for an hour.

Another vegetable dish frequently served is *Ratatouille*, which consists of a good quantity of tomatoes, added to fried aubergines and courgettes, seasoned with salt, pepper and nutmeg and simmered until completely soft and thickened. But, alas, your imported aubergines (egg-plants) have by no means the same taste or consistency as the fresh product.

Of all the meat dishes, I think the *Pot au Feu* is one of the most pleasant and certainly the most economical. But there's no need to give you the recipe, as it's really only a glorified form of Boiled Beef and Carrots with cloves stuck in whole onions to flavour. We are having it tomorrow for dinner, so that I can use up some of the bits for *Tomates Provençales* the next day. With the rest I'll make a *Hachis de Boeuf au Gratin* – which you might also find useful for finishing up left overs.

Start off with the ever present onions browned in oil, followed by two chopped tomatoes, until they form a thick sauce. Then add one or two cups of brown stock, thickened with a little flour, and, after allowing to boil for a few minutes, the cooked meat cut in small pieces. Season, as nearly always, with salt, pepper, nutmeg, parsley and garlic. Turn into a greased oven-proof dish, cover with grated cheese, bread crumbs and dabs of butter, and brown in the oven or under the grill.

By the way, you remarked that your neighbours didn't like being asked for recipes. A good thing they don't live here as everybody exchanges such ideas all the time. It is considered polite to ask for a recipe after sampling a dish. Occasionally, there-fore, someone will say, "You must tell me how it's made', when they don't really care; but usually it's genuine enough. After tonight's *Pistou*, for exam-ple, we are having what I call *Coquilles Madame Roche*, as they are her invention, and she, on the other hand, came over yesterday to ask how I did my meringues.

If I don't mention *Daube*, I know you will. I suppose every Provençal household has its own method, so I can only give you ours. In effect no *Daube* is really good today, as not only is the quality of meat and wine generally inferior these days but formerly the *Daube* was cooked for hours – even days – over the embers of an all wood fire.

However, slightly brown your onions in oil and add a pound of chunked stewing steak and some small pieces of bacon. Cover generously with red wine and, when boiling, put in thyme, bay, salt, pepper and a few diced carrots. Cover and leave over a small light for three hours.

Well, this will only give you a very slight idea of what people here mean by Provençal cooking – not always the same thing as what English cookery books mean by '*à la Provençale*'. For the rest of the dishes, such as *Pieds Paquets* and *Andouillette*, we'll wait for your visit – and it must be a good long one if you want to sample even a cross-section of the possibilities to be served.

25. *Gardening in Provence*

Yes, indeed, the garden grows well. In fact there are moments when everything seems to grow too fast and I don't feel able to keep up. And that, I suppose, is the main answer to your question about the difference of gardening here and in England – the sheer speed of development. Where roses flower in April and dahlias in June, I often find myself disorientated with the seasons, especially the times for planting.

The same, of course, goes for the fruit and vegetables. The 'perpetual' spinach which used to grow in our garden in England lasted, if not perpetually, at least for months on end. Here, despite copious watering, it bolted beyond control after four weeks – before I'd even thought about planting a second row. And although it's very pleasant to pick our plums in the second week of June, I still can't help feeling it's all wrong!

Instead of sowing such vegetables as peas and beans at intervals during spring and summer as in England, here several rows are sown at the same time. It is useless to put such seeds in the earth after the end of April, or the plants will be too young to establish themselves in the face of the heat. On the other hand, when English gardeners have given up peas and beans for the year, here we begin again. Towards the end of August and beginning of September, sowings are made for harvesting in October.

Apart from the necessity of choosing the right phase of the moon, the correct moment for planting in Provence is often quoted by the country folk. For example, last autumn when I asked one of our neighbours whether it was too late to plant rose-bushes, he replied: *'Per Santo Catharino tout bos prend racino.'* (For Saint Catharine all trees take root.) As St. Catharine's feast day falls on November 25th this is a nice way of remarking that trees can safely be moved at a time when all the sap is at its lowest.

Certainly the roses have all done extremely well, but on the other hand our melons presumably failed because I didn't respect the saying: *'Quau vou un bon melounié, lou pagué pèr san José.'* (He who wants a good melon, puts it in the ground for Saint Joseph.) Which is to say, you should plant out about March 19th.

Mind you, as with gardening anywhere, good luck

can often break the rules. Against all correct procedure, we placed strawberry plants at the beginning of May and began to eat the fruit two weeks
later; while an unrooted piece of artichoke plant
which was broken off in April, had its first success
in June, although it shouldn't have shown signs
until October at the earliest – or even the following
year.

I've so far made two outstanding mistakes. The
first was to plant pimentoes instead of green pep-
pers – the seedlings look as alike as do courgettes,
melons and cucumbers. The second was to grow a
magnificent row of broad beans, only to be told that
'while Spaniards may eat them, people here don't'.
The result was a rapid appeal to English acquaintances in the area to come and take their pick.

It would seem that St. Joseph affects not only the
melons but also snails. Old 'Tonton' in Arles (Fernand's uncle) had a favourite saying: *'Per la San José,
li coutards mountro leur bé.'* (For St. Joseph's feast day
the snails show their noses.) In fact the middle of
March does seem to mark the end of snail-winter.

Tonton was always categoric and rarely far
wrong. The figs on the tree by his house appeared to
us to be ripening so well last year that Fernand
remarked we would soon be picking them. 'Not
before July 14th', was the exact reply.

Fernand like his uncle has a fund of quotations
concerning the weather. So for example, 'As Friday,
so Sunday.' 'As the weather for Palm Sunday, so
until St. Michael's feast.' 'If it rains for St. Medard
(June 8th) it rains forty days, unless St. Barnabas
(June 11th) cuts the grass from under his feet.'
'There's never a Saturday without sun.' (Some people add, 'Or at least only one in the year.') 'Satur-

day's wind doesn't go to Monday.' 'Thursday's wind, one, three, six' (days' blowing). 'The Mistral, three, six, nine.'

The Mistral is, of course, a great hazard to gardeners and we are lucky that our patch is both enclosed and facing south. Nevertheless, it is essential to stake a good deal. Even without the wind, the sun dries up the ground in no time at all, so that we have to water every evening – and anything particularly vital in the early morning as well. It is also necessary to use the method of furrowed irrigation in order to hold the moisture at all. Hoeing is the other almost endless activity. Oddly enough, the idea of pithing the ground is unknown here and consequently no light gardening forks are obtainable.

By the way, when people here say '*Jardin*', they mean vegetable garden; the word '*potager*' being understood. The out and out flower garden is a '*Jardin de fleurs*'; or in our case, as there is a goldfish pool and patio incorporated, it is sometimes promoted to '*Jardin d'Agrément*'.

In fact there are few entirely flower gardens here. Perhaps because of the watering problem and perhaps simply because of the time involved for agricultural people who in summer go to the fields at four in the morning and finish the day's work between seven and eight in the evening. Instead there are many flowers grown in pots, particularly geraniums and cacti of many varieties, which can be lifted into the barns during winter.

The rarest flowers of all are the spring bulbs. There are none cultivated in France and the tax on imported bulbs from Holland or England is so high that they become a luxury. It cost me over £2 to buy a handful of narcissi and jonquils, six tulips, two hyacinths and twelve crocus. These latter intrigued our neighbours who, incredibly enough, had never seen a crocus in their lives. They had to come and look closely as the name meant nothing to them either.

In effect the translation of names of quite ordinary flowers has posed me some problems. Some are fairly straightforward. Larkspur, for example, is *Pied d'Alouette* (Lark's Foot). But a Marigold turns into a *Souci* (a Worry), and London Pride becomes The Despair of Artists – for, so they say, no artist has been able to paint one perfectly. The African Marigold changes continents to be known as Indian Rose.

I begin to suspect that when people aren't sure of the correct name of a flower, they call it an *Oeillet* (Carnation) and add some other distinction afterwards. Four such translations I have so far disentangled are:

Stocks, called Carnations of Nice;
Tagetus, called Carnations of India;
Sweet Williams, called Poet's Carnations;
Pinks, called Little Carnations.

Regarding pinks, we are fortunate in having an easy supply of the delicate wild Dianthus, which makes a picture on the rock garden. Other plants which transfer and flourish from the wild include the small pine called Sapinette, honeysuckle, thrift, thyme and especially rosemary: the rosemary cuttings which we placed on arrival already form a sizeable hedge. Which brings me back to my first comment about the speed of development – so I'd better stop and pull out a few more weeds before they, too, grow any bigger!

26. *The Boats of Beaucaire*

Some casual observers assert that all Provençal fêtes are the same but this is far from the case. Certainly, and naturally, there are often some common ingredients – the Majorettes, for example, the drums and fifes or the mounted Gardians – but Provençals are far more aware of, and justly proud of, the local differences.

Thus Tarascon, for instance, is famed for its monster Tarasque and the gun-firing Tartarin. Boulbon has its men-only Procession of the Bottles, which with its libation is almost certainly of pagan origins. Barbentane welcomes the summer solstice with its Fire of St. Jean, which is also a now Christianized tradition of the pagan procedure when the young people jumped across the flames while making vows. At Barjols there is the dance in the church before spit-roasting a beef outside and touring it around on a cart; while Sète has its Water Jousts and Beaucaire draws crowds to see the Arrival of the Merchants by boat for the opening of the Fair.

Although Beaucaire's Fair began in the thirteenth century and remained important until some fifty years ago, its hey-day was in the seventeenth century, when merchants from all over Europe came to sell and buy their wares and up to 800 barques could be seen moored along the quayside. It is this golden era of its history – borne out by documents in its museum – that the town re-creates at the beginning of the annual fair; although nowadays the amusement aspect there dominates.

And it was this re-enactment that caused us the other evening to be walking across the bridge over the Rhône between Tarascon and Beaucaire. We were about half-way when a brass band struck up in the distance, causing consternation to one of two young members of the Réveil Tarasconnais walking behind us.

'They've begun!' he gasped, horror-struck.

'Never mind,' consoled his companion, 'we'll catch them up.' Then after further reflection he added, 'And we won't have to blow so much that way.'

Fernand looked at his watch. It was exactly the advertised hour for commencement of the festivities, but with the wisdom of one born and bred to the time-keeping of the Midi he said, 'It's not beginning. They're just marching up to the assembly point, that's all.' And so, of course, they were.

Beaucaire was in an unusual state of animation. We joined the jostling crowds lining the banks of the canal and manoeuvred past prams, chairs, stools, bicycles and mosquitoes to a position overlooking the quay. There we were wedged between a gregarious Spanish family (the small children, incidentally, speaking French) and a Madame Beaucaire who felt compelled to present her visitors from another department of France to all her acquaintances along the wall. But the lady who attracted most attention and comment was a buxom matron ensconced comfortably on the steps leading down to the water and vehemently refusing to budge an inch to let anyone pass.

Further entertainment was provided throughout the next half-hour by the bewildered drivers of diverted traffic who, reasonably enough since nothing was happening, couldn't understand why they were suddenly not only de-routed but be-jammed.

All this while anxious eyes scanned the dark water for the first sight of the barques, and a small rowing boat used by the organizing authorities raised cheers of frustration at each appearance.

'Until eleven o'clock they won't be there, the boats,' an ice-cream vendor called cheerfully. 'They've not yet arrived. Might as well buy an ice while you wait.'

At last, three quarters of an hour late – which is about the norm – the five bands of the region really began to play and the procession appeared. Led by mounted soldiers of the seventeenth century, wearing wigs and red jackets and carrying standards and authentic long guns, crinolined ladies walked beside gentlemen with triangular hats. The bands massed in formations on the quayside and a display was given. Perhaps this was an evocation of the days when acrobats and clowns tried out their acts at Beaucaire before taking the open roads of Europe; but as the ordinary lighting was poor and the flood-lighting equivocal, it was difficult to see.

The crowd applauded none the less and even more so when an apparent barrage of muskets from the bridge over the canal turned into a firework cascade and the water was further illuminated by red, green and white flares. But where, oh where, were the boats?

The question was still being asked when the pro-

cession turned away from the canal towards the
arena for the official opening of the Fair. This is also
proclaimed throughout streets with names such as
the Road of the Jewellers, where formerly nothing
but jewellery was sold. We followed the crowd for a
way and then stopped to chat with a present-day
trader of the town. Presently we asked about the
boats.

'No boats this year,' he said. And then, seeing our
amazement, he explained with what to him was perfect logic. 'They had the fireworks instead, you see.'

All of which goes to show that not only are all
Provençal fêtes not the same, but that not even are
they necessarily the same each year in any given
town.

27.   Châteaurenard's
Charrette

The charrette about which you've read is a summer
phenomenon of Provence. Sometimes I wonder for
how many summers it can continue, for the charrette is a decorated cart drawn by horses or mules,
and each year there are less horses and mules to be
found. Formerly almost every village had its charrette which was paraded for the local feast day but
nowadays there are far fewer; and there is a good
deal of animal-lending in order to make even these
possible.

Not so very long ago, Boulbon, for example, had

its charrette; for, not so very long ago, there were a hundred horses at work in the fields of Boulbon. Now there is just one left. His name is Coco and he is now over twenty years old. We met him recently pulling a plough for his master to furrow between the vines, so we stopped to watch and to listen. To my ears, the particular language of sing-song cries used to guide such horses as remain at work, have a remarkable resemblance to the cries used to indicate direction by the gondoliers of Venice. Man and beast were both glad to pause when they next came to the turn by us.

'He's a great horse, Coco,' said his master, as he carefully adjusted the hat which protected the animal's ears, 'but, like me, he's not so young as he was.'

We asked if he'd replace Coco when he could no longer work, but he thought it would probably have to be a tractor.

'I suppose it's progress,' he sighed doubtfully and he went on to recall the past horses of Boulbon and the lost charrette.

However, among the charrettes that do continue traditionally, there is still a choice of type. There is the racing charrette of St. Eloi at Graveson, for instance; the stately charrette of St. Roch at Rognonas with mounted Arlesiennes; St. Rémy's with donkeys included; Châteaurenard's with the singing whips.

Châteaurenard's patronal festival being St. Mary Magdalene's day at the end of July, in full fruit season, and Châteaurenard being one of the most important fruit growing centres, one is there assured of plenty of melons, plums, apples, peaches, pears and the early 'Madeleine' grapes to decorate this cart (there is also another for St. Eloi). But its most outstanding aspect is that by tradition each driver in turn plays airs on his whip; so Château-renard's charrette was the one we chose to see this year.

The essential part of such an outing is not just to see the cart go by but to experience the general atmosphere of expectation, so in good time we were merged into the dense crowds cramming the Course, which was lined by the market booths as far as the corner of the fun-fair. Stalls offered everything from sweets, via the heavy petanque bowls and agricultural machinery, to clothing of every type.

Any purchaser automatically becomes a focal point of interest for all immediate passers-by and what he buys or leaves is generally noted and discussed. A lady struggles to try on a dress over the one she is wearing. Too big? Perhaps. Try another. That's better. Hair ruffled and a bit out of breath with all that effort in the heat, she proffers twenty francs to the vendor.

'But no, Madame. The price is twenty-nine.'

'It says twenty on the notice,' she insists and is backed up by the person beside her.

But when the notice is held up clear of the pile of dresses, sure enough there is the tail of the nine. The selected item is regretfully replaced and the crowd, waiting with interest for the outcome, moves on.

It is time to get into position for the charrette. But which way will it come? Nobody is sure. Some years it begins from a Mas on the route to Eyragues; others it comes from the quarter of La Crau. After all, it doesn't much matter, since one way or the other it passes all the principal streets of the town.

We were lucky enough to find a table outside a

bar, where at least we had our heads in the shade. Our feet meanwhile grilled in full sun and people standing in the shade on the other side of the street didn't know whether to be relieved that they were not therefore burning, or envious of the fact that we were sitting down. One lady came to the perfect compromise by marching across the road, helping herself to a chair from inside the café and carrying it back to her patch of shade on the pavement opposite.

Then, as a solitary policeman sauntered down the road, whistle in mouth, and held up a laconic hand to already confused traffic, the procession arrived.

The first cart bore the local band; accent on youth, more merry than tuneful – but who minds that in the heat? Next an escort of ridden horses, followed by the twenty-five caparisoned horses and mules pulling the famous charrette. Fruit in abundance – even one apple on a string at the back, which the children tried to seize – and a mass of glorious red gladioli, heads of which were thrown with confetti into the crowd.

And then the men with their whips that we'd come to see and hear. There were four of them this year taking it in turns to create their tunes from crack and lash. Hard enough to do at any time, but doubly so while walking the hot streets beside their not always docile beasts.

The crowd clapped and the charrette continued its way, leaving the inevitable discussions behind.

'Should be all horses and no mules,' snorted one old man. 'There were a hundred horses when I was a boy.'

'And where would you find them now?' came the rejoinder. 'Before long we'll be down to tractors drawing the charrette.'

We thought of that one last horse of Boulbon and agreed.

'Moreover, there'll soon be no one left who can play the whip,' grumbled the first speaker. 'One year here I heard a recognizable Marseillaise.'

But most of the crowd was content with the charrette. Enough animals had somehow been found; Châteaurenard had held to its tradition and – Marseillaise or no– the whips had been played.

28. Wine Ways

I'm glad you enjoyed your Tavel at the dinner party. I suppose it's the best – and is certainly the best known –of the rosé wines of Provence. We generally have a few bottles in the house for special occasions and were recently over at the Tavel Cave, where, incidentally, the concierge is an ex-prisoner-of-war acquaintance of Fernand's. There's certainly no reason why you shouldn't visit these cellars when you come down, since you are interested. Numbers of people are shown round every year.

But last week we were replenishing supplies of three of the many excellent wines of the region less talked about than Tavel: all rouge, as that is our general preference. The first has a grand name for what, at least we think, is a grand wine, Royal Provence. Its label reads, *'Rouge pour le Roti. Grand Vin Mousseux. Méthode Champenoise."*

It does indeed go well with the roast, or any other meat, and makes an admirable change from the more expensive and heavier Châteauneuf du Pape or Gigondas for that purpose. Unfortunately nearly the whole output of this sparkling and most digestible red is exported – mostly to Germany – leaving the white mousseux for French consumption. However as we have friends in Rognac, where this is made (some sixty kilometres north of Marseille) we are able to combine a visit to them and the Cave from time to time.

The other wines aren't even bought from cellars. They are sold in Bellegarde – but if the name Bellegarde only conjures up for you the famous *blanc de clairette* of that region, come with us in the car to a somewhat curious destination.

En route we cross the recently finished Pont d'Aramon. It is new and it is useful but the sentimentalist can't help regretting the old wooden ferry with its precarious-looking pulley, which used to make an adventure here of crossing the Rhône. He will be horrified, too, by what industry is doing to the area.

For the moment, Aramon is an attractive and quite sizeable village with a sixteenth-century church and town hall. Not only does it have a habitable castle but a chemist's – sign of some importance: our village has neither doctor nor chemist.

We pass by Montfrin, which has an even more imposing castle. According to tradition, St. Louis stayed here before he set sail on his crusade from Aigues-Mortes. It is certainly now true that an eminent French statesman passes his holidays here, as his family owns this castle – which mostly dates from the fifteenth to eighteenth centuries but includes a

Saracen tower.

And so on to Jonquières, whose castle-like building turns out to be the Mairie. There is a street called after Alphonse Daudet, whose story of the two inns of St. Vincent you'll doubtless remember. St. Vincent is on the main route to Nîmes but Daudet included Jonquières as one of the three places from which the young people came to 'the inn across the road'.

Finally to Bellegarde, where we draw up outside an old Mas on the road to Beaucaire. Two large acacias dominate the courtyard where flowers tumble in happy disorder across the pathway. The last vestiges of grey paint cling to the railings and gate but there is no indication that this is anything other than a private residence. The only notice says, 'Chien Méchant' and this is soon given the lie by three miniscule and merrily welcoming terriers.

However, a paper on the open door of the barn shows the prices of various wines. Fernand comments out loud on the rising costs.

'Yes,' comes an unexpected voice from the darkness of the interior, 'but the worst is the one that's gone up in francs and down to a three-quarter litre bottle.'

The speaker is a jovial old man in a check cloth cap and a faded blue shirt anchored by an outsize safety-pin. Grey trousers are held up over a well-rounded middle by both braces and belt; and although this is said to be one definition of a pessimist, nobody could be less of a one than he. Leaning on a stick to support a leg three times broken, and speaking Patois more easily than French, he keeps up a light-hearted banter while passing out the bottles required.

In the dark cobwebbery of a former heavily beamed stable we nearly stumbled over the cage of a black pheasant indignantly pacing inside. To reach the simple racks of bottles we negotiate barrels as old as the building and the tail of an outsize peacock unaccountably squashed in the jam of the door. I ask if it's a habitual haunt and the old man mutters darkly, 'Ought to be put in prison that bird,' and goes on counting bottles.

Bottles of what? you'll be asking. Wines of various types but all with one thing in common on their label: *'N. D. de Neiges. La Bastide. Lozère.'* How it all started, nobody seems quite clear but the monks of this Trappist monastery of Our Lady of Snows in the Lozère own acres of vineyards here in Bellegarde. Every year two brothers travel south to select and supervise the harvesting of the grapes and their subsequent processing, but there are also four laymen to help in the white Cave across the road surmounted by its statue of Our Lady.

After about six months all the quality wines are moved up to mature for three years in the cool monastery cellars among the hills of Lozère. This is the secret of the wine's success, and this is why we go to Bellegarde to buy the apéritif Muscat and the tonic Cassagnas.

The ordinaire wines don't go up to the mountains but are excellent all the same. Such is the twelve degree rosé which the old man presses us to taste. At first we refuse but when I catch the expression on his face and say, 'You'd like to as well,' he winks and hurries to draw a glassful from the barrel via an ancient rubber tube.

This guardian vendor of the monks' wine is eighty-one years old and has been installed there for as long as Fernand can remember. Despite the lack of advertisement or notices, the wines are widely known and there is an all-day long procession of buyers. The old man is interested in all-comers and their families and homes but there is an extra broad smile for those speaking Provençal.

Last year he had an operation and when the surgeon made the routine checks he said, 'No need to worry. You'll live to be a hundred.'

'I'll sign for that,' the old man replied. And nobody who knows him will be surprised to find him celebrating his century among the bottles in the barn.

29. *Provençal and Patois*

You say I've confused the issue for you by mentioning both Patois and a language of Provençal. I'm sorry but it's not surprising as there's a good deal of confusion over the the subject here. Provençal is indeed a language in its own right, with its literature and grammar and its chair in universities of various countries – although perhaps the most important centre naturally remains at Aix-en-Provence.

It is a language which had its hey-day at the time of Roi René, the Troubadours and the Courts of Love, and it is a language which in the nineteenth century was corrupted to the point of becoming moribund. Then it was, on May 21st, 1854 to be precise, that seven poets met together in the Château of Fontségune, near Avignon, and founded the famous association called the Félibrige. Everyone asks what the name signifies and nobody seems to be able to give an answer; apart from the fact that the word was taken from a popular old song.

Frederic Mistral became the most renowned of these seven poets and he probably did the most towards resuscitating and purifying Provençal, which was the avowed aim of the association. Not only did he write and get accepted by Parisian audiences the two plays which have since become classics, Mirèio (Mireille) and Calendau (Christmas), but he also set about producing a clarified grammar and dictionary of Provençal.

The problem is that obviously this very correct language is not strictly that spoken by the people; especially as reading is here a very rare pastime. The idea was to teach the children this proper version but unfortunately (as I've already mentioned) due to so many pressures and difficulties the effort has not been widespread. The schoolchildren of St. Rémy, for example, study Provençal for one hour each week: those at Tarascon not at all.

The result is that older people, knowing that their version of the language is not a hundred per cent the 'proper Provençal', invariably refer to themselves as speaking Patois. And in a sense they are right. Basically it is the Provençal of the Félibrige but over the course of the years many corruptions (and distortions of French words) have crept in. To make matters worse there are variations on the theme from village to village: a word or expression

currently used in Barbentane or Boulbon, for
instance, may not be the same in Graveson or Maillane.

And not infrequently the vocabulary used in written Provençal is unknown to ordinary people. Often
I've heard the villagers complaining that they don't
understand all the expressions used by local broad-
casters or journalists; while Fernand, who spent all
his youth either in Châteurenard or Arles and thus
speaks what he calls Patois fluently, has several
times been floored by words in the book from which
I am trying to study Provençal.

For me the rub is inverted. Having begun by
taking the academic approach, I find Provençal easy
enough to read and can generally understand well
enough what is said – but all the variations tongue-tie
any hope of joining in a conversation. Moreover, I
am still often at a loss to distinguish whether a word
is Provençal, French, Patois or Slang.

People here hotly deny that Provençal has anything in common with Portuguese or Spanish, but
inevitably, being a Latin-based tongue, it has, and
this is often an aid to disentangling meanings. Mind
you, there are not a few words akin to English, such
as Cauleflore (Cauliflower) and Cat (hence the
simple name of ours).

During the past half century many Italians have
become integrated with the people of this region
and this has had a certain bearing on the language –
or should we say patois? Incidentally, it is odd to
think that while fifty years ago these Italians (almost
all originating from the same village of Santa Maria
da Monte) were naturally referred to as 'the
foreigners' by the Provençals – now it is they who,
completely part of their surroundings, use the term

'foreigners' for the increasing numbers of Spaniards coming here to settle.

But to return to Frédéric Mistral and all he did for the Provençal language, you should one day visit the Museon Arlatan in Arles. This was founded by Mistral with the money from the Nobel Prize which he won in 1907, and among the many rooms showing different aspects of Provençal life and history is a section devoted to the Félibrige.

Then, as a complement to that, we must also take you to the little village of Maillane, where Mistral was born and lived and died. The Mas du Juge, where he was born, is not always open to the public but, with its flock of sheep making a picturesque foreground beside the long avenue of trees, it is worth passing by on the road to St. Rémy. Each time I do so I remember the frustrating occasion when a performance of *Calendau* in the forecourt was completely outblown by the Mistral (wind, not poet!) but it did at least give me the chance to go in and see the old hall with the inscriptions above the fireplace.

Mirèio was finished when Frédéric was living in the house in the village known as the Maison du Lézard. Above the sundial on the façade, dated 1903, is written:

"Gái lesert, beu toun souleu,
l'ouro passo que trop lèu
e deman pléura belèu."

Gay lizard, how beautiful your sun,
time passes only too quickly
and tomorrow it may rain.

Opposite this is the rather lugubrious-looking, shrub-shrouded building where Mistral lived from 1876 to 1914. Except on Tuesdays, this is regularly

open to visitors, who find their way in through a weedy garden of tattered yews, pines and palms, by following various arrows marked 'Gardien'.

This guardian has been in charge for the past twenty-five years and much laments that comparatively few people (more foreigners than French) come to the house – which the poet made over to the municipality of Maillane. He had caused it to be built when, at the age of forty-two, he married, so it is fitting that above each side of the grey marble fireplace in the salon should hang two large portraits of himself and his wife. One wonders whether it was she, only nineteen at the time of the wedding, who played the small upright piano and who embroidered the tapestry covering some of the furniture.

Mistral's books, manuscripts and letters are displayed here but one feels closer to the author in his study on the other side of the hall. In contrast to the elaborate tiled-floor of the salon, the study has a plain parquet, which is not only rare in Provence but was considered a great luxury in Mistral's day. He worked at a remarkably narrow desk, having nine drawers above and five below. Among the books in his library is a biography of La Reine Jeanne, whose mausoleum near Les Baux he had copied ready for his own burial in the peaceful little cemetery just along the road from his house. On the wall by the entrance is a quotation from *Mirèio* including the line: 'Death is life!'

The bedroom where Mistral died has been left untouched. A single bed with walnut head and frame shows that he did not share this room with his wife. The now faded wallpaper is heavily floral but the furniture is simple – a washstand with blue patterned jug and bowl, a 'Margote' or 'vide-poche' for small objects, four straw-seated chairs, a tall bedside table and a chest-of-drawers with a Crucifix and statue of Our Lady of Graces, to whom the church at Millane is dedicated. Incidentally, it was Mistral who donated the baroque style white marble altar to this church.

In the afternoons the poet took his siesta on an extraordinarily small and hard bed, more like a doctor's couch, in a room overlooking the garden towards the Alpilles. Here, too, is placed the large wardrobe, also of walnut as is all old Provençal furniture.

Some of the people who today spend fortunes

buying so-called Provençal dining-rooms, con-
sisting of table, chairs and sideboards, would be
astonished to see the reality such as it is in Mistral's
house. Fixed on one wall is a beautifully carved
wooden 'Paniero' for the bread, flanked by two
decorated boxes for matches and for salt. Beneath
these is the small sideboard called a 'Credence';
while on the other side of the table stands the 'Pas-
tiero' used for kneading the bread, or occasionally
for salting meat.

The size of the 'Oulo', the vast copper soup-
tureen, gives some idea of the copious meals served
in the past and it is easy to imagine this room
resounding with the piquant conversations of the
assembled Félibrige. Certainly it is due to their
most illustrious member Mistral that Maillane is
still today the village where Patois and Provençal
come the nearest to being the same.

30. Bicyclettes, Boules, Belote

Probably you see much more of the Tour de France
on television than we do from the side of the road.
In fact unless one is an avid follower of the race
from start to finish, it is not particularly exciting just
to see the straining streams of competitors panting
by. Often an equally intense and far more amusing
atmosphere surrounds the local Course de Bicyclet-
tes organized in conjunction with village festivities.

There was one such here last week, which not only

began and finished in the main square but passed through the village no less than six times at half-hourly intervals. Thus there was a chance to identify the competitors and compare their progress each time round – and in between whiles the spectators could make their criticisms, exchange other news and have a quick drink at the café.

Each appearance of the hurtling bicycles was heralded by police, accompanied by trainers, followed by the sweeping-up-cum-first-aid van and commented upon excitedly by the organizers over a very loud speaker. While the cyclists were sweating their way round several other villages in the area, people came forward to offer extra prizes for each lap. For instance, the leader of the first time round, whom we never again noticed, had at least the consolation of a pound of a well-known brand of coffee for his pains.

For the young, there is great glamour in the *'coureur'* or professional racing cyclist, but not too much chance of emulation. On the other hand, there cannot be a boy in Provence who doesn't start competing in Boules (even if only with his small friends) as soon as he can hold and throw the bowls. Indeed during most local fêtes there are special events held for the juniors, using lighter-weight bowls than the normal heavier metal variety.

Maybe you are having visions of bowls played on English lawns by white-dressed ladies and blazered gentlemen, but these have little in common with Boules or, to use the correct name, Petanque. For one thing lawns are almost nonexistent in Provence and Petanque is played on any open patch of ground – admittedly tidied up a bit for competitions. The rougher the ground the more sporting the chances, and here at home we play a satisfactory if sometimes infuriating game along the cart-track beside the Mas. As far as 'uniform' among competitors is concerned, the recognized outfit of a genuine Provençal boulomane consists of well-worn trousers, cap and espadrilles.

Boules can be played *'tête à tête'*, i.e. by two players, but it is a much better game with competing couples. One of each is the *'pointeur'* and the other the *'tireur'*. Both use the jerky underarm flick-throw to begin with but the pointer's bowl then runs along the ground to position close to the *'bouchon'*, or white marker ball, while the tireur's throw is intended to land on top of an opponent's bowl and so displace it from an advantageous place.

But it would need a book instead of a letter to explain and describe all the ins and outs of Petanque – and as an initiate outsider I wouldn't get far in the job, for there are so many nuances and special terms (a *'Fanny'*, for example, for no points gained). The broad outline is that the first to reach fifteen (or sometimes thirteen) points wins the game: that's to say, fifteen bowls counted as being nearest to the marker after all players have thrown. (The order of throwing being determined by the distances measured.)

But the joy for the spectators is not only the game but the intensity and variety of expressions and positions of the players. That tense moment as the distance between two bowls and the marker is measured, could never be conveyed in writing; no more than the long-drawn pause while a player reflects from which angle to send his bowl.

Comments from players and spectators alike are usually terse, to the point and often of wry humour.

Recently we overheard one spectator advising his partner: 'Don't look at the marker; look at me.'

To which came the reply: 'You're mad. If I look at you, I'm completely undone.'

Then: 'Let me play the way I want to. If you don't stop advising me, it'll be my head that spins instead of the bowl.'

And when a player, who having thrown away his chance, moaned aloud, 'Oh what an idiot I am', the Captain of his team remarked, 'His judgement is always sure.'

Another competitor making one mistake after another, drew from a friend in the crowd, 'Come on now. Stop hiding your game from the opponents and show them you can play bowls.'

But of course all these asides lose their flavour once translated.

When joints begin to grow stiff with age, one can still play what is nicely known as Tired Boules with one's older companions, but age doesn't affect ability to play *Belote*, that great card game of the Midi. If a villager says, 'I'm just going to the café,' it often means, 'I'm just going to play *Belote*'; for the café is the equivalent of a club for the men.

Fernand plays *Belote* instinctively but for all his explanations I still get bogged down in the mathematics of the affair. For only certain cards of the pack are used and the values are different from those to which we are accustomed. The Jack and nine of trumps are the most valuable cards, although the *Belote* itself is formed by the King and Queen of trumps.

Not that it matters that I can't follow all the intricacies. For one thing it is essentially a man's game and, for another, the outsiders' greatest

pleasure is once more simply in watching. To sit
in a quiet corner while the game progresses is to
see the essence of Cézanne's famous 'Card Players'
spring to life. More than that, it is to become in some
measure attuned to the springs of life in Provence.

31.   Fruit Funeral

'Can you stand bad smells? There's no point in
coming if not,' said our fruit grower neighbour.
Being short-handed, he had come to ask Fernand
to drive one of two lorry-loads of pears.

'To the market?'

'To be thrown away,' came the terse reply.

Two lorry-loads of perfect pears representing
months of work and careful supervision. Now
several more hours were needed – to throw
them away.

We drove the twenty kilometres to the large market at Châteaurenard, which opens daily at six
o'clock in the morning. Came the verification: the
price of pears having for three days been lower than
the basic price fixed by the Common Market, this
fruit which could not be sold might then be thrown
away.

After waiting in a long line of lorries, we received
permission for our loads to be disposed of, and the
two vehicles were then weighed. A tedious tour
through the traffic of the town took us to the headquarters of the Groupement de Producteurs, where

a note was made and signed of the loads to be thrown away. A further winding way was then negotiated to the place of discharge – a desolate, dried-up bed of the River Durance.

The smell reached us before we were actually there but even that could not prepare the imagination for what was to come. Never the expression 'the mind boggled' could have been more apt. The further we progressed, the more I felt engulfed by a Gulliverian sense of unreality.

To reach the main tip we slushed through a black sea of what looked like ink but which proved to be the liquefied remains of countless tons of potatoes On, through clouds of dust and flies, past mound upon mound of mouldering fruit – pears, plums, apricots, tomatoes, peaches. One grower alone tipped 400 cases, in a week when peaches sold for five new pennies a piece in London.

We were late, so that only about eighty lorries remained on the vast dumping site – quite enough to imprint a nightmare scene on the memory. Vehicles were parked at all angles, wherever a corner in the stinking morass could be found. As in some scene from Dante's Inferno, one had the impression of arms; hundreds of sunburnt arms, tipping ton after ton of first-class fruit from the sides, the backs, the doors, the windows of lorries. There was a horrid rhythm in the chaos; arms down to pick up a crate, arms outstretched to empty its contents, arms sideways to throw the receptacle back on a pile. And this multiplied in all directions as far as the unbelieving eye could see.

I wanted to cry, 'Stop! It's not true. Let me wake up.' But with the implacable relentlessness of a huge machine out of control, the work of destruction continued. Men sweated in the heat in near silence among this wanton waste. The normal loud voices of the Midi were muted. No smiles: no handshakes: none of the usual crackling conversational exchanges.

Our first lorry sank helplessly into a patch of pulp which a bulldozer had tried to cover with pebbles from the river-bed. A chain was produced and the vehicle towed out by another grower from our village who happened to be beside. It was a matter of fact procedure, with none of the badinage frequently heard on such occasions. It was happening all round: it happened again as the front wheel sank into the squelchy mass of pulped pear: it happened to us with a wheel spinning senselessly in a putrified purée of potato.

Somehow the disorganized procession of fruit hearses disentangled itself from this repulsive malodorous, soul-destroying Slough of Despond. Lorries were re-weighed in the market-place; cards controlled yet once more by the office and eventually we were on the way home, with nostrils and vehicle still full of that all-pervading smell.

This was the seventh journey made by our neighbour to the dump this season, and there will be several more. It will be at least six or seven months before he will receive a governmental pittance averaging twenty centimes per kilo for throwing away his fruit. His immediate alternatives are to pay either for cold storage or forced ripening. In neither case can it be guaranteed that the fruit will fetch enough to cover cost.

And if that were the only cost it would be nothing. The five tons of pears we threw away this morning have been an endless source of expenditure and effort since last autumn, when the ground round the trees was first worked. This was subsequently repeated five or six times. Pruning took place in winter, followed by the collection and burning of the branches cut. Precautions against frost were necessary and the trees have been sprayed against insects and fungus on fourteen occasions.

Two big weeding operations were needed during the year and watering according to weather conditions. As the pears ripened they were thinned; the weaker fruit being plucked out by hand. Finally the fruit-pickers had to be paid – plus tax, insurance, paper and packing crates. We spent a vast sum on petrol alone this morning. All this for what? To be told to go and throw the result of all these overheads and months of labour into an old bed of the Durance.

What is wrong? These particular pears are of a large variety appreciated by the public – tasty, juicy. Without detriment they can be forced or frozen. They travel as far as required without damaging. So the fault does not lie there. There is talk of governmental desire to remove 80,000 agricultural units from the French fields, so that the policy of exporting industrial material and importing fruit and vegetables from less advanced countries may be pursued. There is talk of flooding the market by fruit from Italy, where the cost of production is lower. There is talk of unfair balance of payments somewhere along the selling line of merchants, wholesalers and retailers – pears in the shops here are still selling at nearly two francs the kilo. But talk doesn't mend.

It is not as if the dump to which we went is unique.

It is only one of the dumps in one department. It is estimated that in the neighbouring department of the Vaucluse, 40,000 tons of fruit have already been thrown away this season.

If the fruit-growers themselves cannot crystallize what needs to be done, it is certainly not for an outsider to judge. However, one thing is abundantly clear: there's something so rotten in this state of affairs, that it's not only the fruit that smells.

32. *Historical Heritage*

Your remark that I haven't told you the history of the Mas, coincided with a meeting this week with 'Monsieur the Historian', whom you will remember from 'Life in Provence'. Since we moved here he has been interesting himself in the history of the house, spending long hours among the necessary archives, and yesterday he told us the results of his searchings.

In effect it has still not been possible to trace exactly when the second part of the building was constructed, with its oddly marked rafters made from old boats of the Rhône; but the earlier section was in existence before 1409. Then it was mentioned as being the Mas by the communal sheep pasturage in the area known as the Claux (Enclosure) de Courpil. Although it is no longer a communal grazing ground, sheep frequently continue to pasture in the fields behind here today. In 1409 there was already a roadway opposite and a cabanon beside. The Mas belonged to Girant Rigant who sold it to Marsio Berenger.

From the roof levels it is easy to see the extent of Rigant's house, which includes what today is part of the Mas next door. In fact one of our rooms goes underneath one of their bedrooms, and the enormous hook once used for hanging pigs is so firmly embedded between our ceiling and their floor that it was too risky to move. Here there is still the original fourteenth-century vaulting but unfortunately a much larger version in the adjacent room was beyond restoration.

Between the two was a tumbledown wall with an entrance only possible to pass by bending double. The same applied to the outer doorway, because, due to repeated inundations of the Rhône, the levels have changed. In the central stone above the inner doorway was carved a heart with the date 1733. Who was in love at this point? The shepherd, the pig-keeper, or the baker? For by this time a large oven had been installed – an oven which, fortunately for us, caused a court case and thus added to the written history of the house.

Few notifications are extant for the previous 300 years. In 1561 the Mas belonged to someone from Arles; in 1643 the '*Bourgeois sieur Jean Bourg*' bought it from the 'Dame Comtesse'. This Countess was Madame Julie de Fortin de la Roque, who later bought the Seigneurie of Boulbon (then known as Bourbon).

By 1661 Jean Bourg's son, Pierre, had become a noble and the Mas had a garden as well as such a large area of land that Pierre had to pay 'seventy livres six sols' in annual taxation – an enormous sum for those days. Maybe he found it too much to keep up as by 1701 he had sold to the 'Seigneur Presi-dent'. As this meant the President of the Parliament of Aix-en-Provence, the outcome of the case of the oven could have been in no doubt.

At this time it was obligatory for everyone in a commune to take their bread to be baked in the village oven but owners of an outlying Mas could apply for permission to construct their own ovens, and this is what the President did. Subsequently it became a '*four banal*', which is to say that all the bread for the neighbourhood was baked there. The chimney, now blocked up, rises beside the original fourteenth-century stone spiral staircase, while the stone shelves for the bread stretched below what is now the main staircase.

The President did not live here himself as he had a *'rentier'*, who worked the lands and divided the gains with his proprietor, and it is probable that his son Raoulx de Raousset continued the same system, since he was also *'Seigneur et Comte de Bourbon'*. Thus he would have had the choice of the splendid castle on the hill for his domain, or what is known as the *'Maison Basse'*, which is just along the road from here.

None of our neighbours could explain why this large building with its gargoyle decorations should be called the 'Low House' when, as they pointed out, it is the highest and most important house in the area. Now Monsieur the Historian explains that for the Lords of Boulbon it was the house low down in the plain, as opposed to the castle on the Montagnette.

After the Revolution, Raoulx's son, Emile Raousset, necessarily dropped his title and the preposition, and almost certainly lived in this Mas. Possibly it was he who enlarged the house, for an act of 1791 mentioned not only the land he possessed by the Mas and, for the first time, the yard, but also his brother Aurelle Raousset, who then became the owner. Furthermore, on the next official map to be made the house was named for the first time as Le Pigeonnier – a name which has gradually been used to include the whole neighbourhood.

In 1837 Aurelle divided the Mas between two men, perhaps his sons-in-law. Then the more recent names include several still held by some of our neighbours, including a Commandant who

ordered a new staircase in the rose-beige Tavel
stone and the white marble chimney-piece in
our bedroom.

Sitting under the heavy beams by the big open
fireplace in the livingroom, we sometimes wonder
about these our predecessors. Who had forged the
iron fireback with its image of the guardian angel
leading the soul from the clutches of the devil? The
same person who placed the statue of the *Sacré Coeur*
in the façade? Who sat under the plane-tree and
dipped his plume in the earthen ink-well which
Fernand dug up entire and still clearly varnished?
Who first cooked under the big chimney in the
barn? Who used, broke and threw away the black
medieval pottery, known to have been fired in a
village not far from here, which comes to light as I
hoe the vegetable plot? And who, more recently,
dropped the two-centime piece of 1858 found in the
flower bed?

Last June, as we stood watching the flames of the
'*Feu de St. Jean*' traditionally lit outside our Mas,
there was a sense of historical continuity with all
these unknown people of the past.

'Our forebears lit the fire as a protection for their
sheep against the gall,' explained one lady, who
presumably didn't know about the earlier pagan
custom of leaping across the flames.

Her forebears had done it and that was enough.
Her forebears, who were in fact owners of our
house. And before them?

'This fire has been lit for as long as anyone here
can remember', she insisted.

Nowadays, as the person opposite is called Jean,
the occasion is linked with the neighbourhood cal-
ling to wish him a happy feast day. Accordingly we

all gathered in the road at 9.30 p.m. and went in Indian file to shake his hand and present a plant or bunch of flowers. It was interesting to note that as we sat round the table for coffee and home-made liqueurs, all the men were ranged on one side of the room and the women on the other (as still is the case in the village church).

The men talked hunting, fishing and politics: the women, cooking, children and sewing. Then outside again for that solemn moment of putting a match to the pile of faggots. In near silence we watched the flames mount in the still warm air of the summer night – fourteen people from Le Pigeon-nier linked by historical heritage with those who called the same place the Claux de Courpil.

33. *Oil of the Country*

I remember telling you that we buy grape-pip oil from Bagnols-sur Cèze for general use in cooking, as we find it lighter than ground-nut oil and less strongly flavoured than either that or the sunflower variety. All the same, it is a pleasant luxury from time to time to use real olive oil for the salad dressing. Not so long ago, all Provençal cooking was done in olive oil but its present high cost and the usually inferior quality of the commercial product have caused a change in habit, except among some of the older generation.

All this to say that last Saturday saw us in Beau-

caire at the co-operative olive-mill, which is directed
by a friend of Fernand's. He met us outside the grey
building, with its splendid, uninterrupted view
across to the best preserved part of the Fort St.
André, and he explained that all the rocky land
behind also belonged to the oleiculteurs. Then as
we went through the gates past the notice 'Sale of
Olive Oil of the Country' into the courtyard, he
commented that they'd had to make a one-way
system in order to de-block the long lines of olive-
bearing carts waiting to unload at the mill.

Between the beginning of November and the
middle of January, olives arrive here every afternoon, brought mostly by the growers from the
Gard. The industry in this area crescendoed after
the turn of the century, when many acres of land
were planted with olive trees instead of vines, and
there are still fifteen mills in the heart of Provence.
The Nyons' olive is reputed to be the best and admittedly the fruit is larger (and therefore gives a higher
yield of oil), but the Director at Beaucaire insisted
that his oil has a better taste. Certainly we've
throughly enjoyed every mouthful of salad these
past few days.

The olives brought to Beaucaire are all green and
mostly of the Picholine variety; so that it takes a
hundred kilos to yield eighteen litres of oil. Imagine
great mounds of these green, pebble-like fruit being
unloaded in the courtyard and hoisted by a pulley
up to a granary, stacked high. To reach it we
mounted a rickety iron spiral staircase which served
its youth in the Beaucaire arena.

As the olives arrive their tonnage is noted, for,
this being a co-operative, the oil is distributed to the
growers according to the amount of fruit turned in.

Then they are scooped up with long-handled shovels into large iron buckets by one of the five workmen on duty. Throughout the 'Campaign', as it is called, two teams work ten hours each. Several of the men are ex-prisoners, or those saved from prison by the good offices of the Director, who in this way helps them to begin life again. One young man, well on the way to becoming a hardened criminal, is now a happily married and well-balanced individual.

The filled buckets are fixed onto black bars running round the granary, so that with a flick of the wrist they can be sent crazily crashing and clanging, like some ancient Giant Dipper, to the corner where there is most space for storage. Then, in order to begin their transformation into oil, the olives are shovelled into a chute leading through a funnel into the presses.

Originally when this mill was opened in 1926 the press consisted of two enormous round stones, similar to the grindstones for flour. Now there are four modern machines – all from Italy and two of them quite recent. The consternation caused when these last two arrived from Italy, was vividly recalled by the Director. Awaited urgently, with olives overflowing the yard, they were not the machines expected. Not only were they very expensive but also necessitated other material and a return to the system of 'Scourtins', not required by the two former machines.

The administration spent all night debating in the draughty office but when the morning light again showed the piles of waiting olives, they decided to raise a loan and keep the presses. The members themselves then installed the machines on a temporary, rather Heath Robinson, basis. But temporary installations in Provence not infrequently become permanent fixtures, and the presses remain shored up but extremely efficient today.

A 'Scourtin' is a round mat with a hole in the centre for its positioning, through which the pulp is passed. Formerly these were made of coconut but nowadays nylon is used as it is easier to clean. We felt ourselves most fortunate to be able to buy one of the few remaining fibre Scourtins, which now makes a most attractive mat in the sitting-room.

The pressing of the pulp takes about a quarter of an hour and the oil (known at this point as the 'Oil of Hell') is purified in water, heated by a large stove standing in the outsize old cowled chimney-place. Another delightfully old-fashioned tall stove, of the type which used to heat English village schoolrooms and railway stations, burns day and night during the winter to prevent the storage tanks of oil from freezing. A further relic is the system of large wooden wheels below the ceiling, which have always been used to work the pulley; only that today it is turned by a machine instead of hand.

Altogether this mill is an example of how old and new can harmonize. It handles an average of 150,000 kilos of olives in a season, and distribution to contributors only is made for Christmas cooking, although the oil is not yet matured.

Few of the oleiculteurs draw their full quota of oil, which enables the rest to be sold directly to the public. We wondered who came to buy it in this unpublicized, out of the way corner of Beaucaire.

'Lovers of oil from all over the place,' came the Director's reply. 'That lady who has just left lives in the Ardèche but people come from as far away as

Lyon, Paris and even Lille. Most of the oil sold is for
table use but there is also a steady market for
medicinal purposes.'

When one realizes that the greater part of commercial olive oil is made with chemicals from the
leftover *pâte* (known as the Grignon) of mills like
this one, it's not surprising that people will go out of
their way to find the natural product – or Virgin Oil
as it is called. The Grignon is also used in soap
manufacture; while the remains of the pulp can be
sold for cattle food and certain types of fertilizer.

While we were talking, the Vice-President of the
society came in. He is a smiling, sprightly man of
eighty-two, who has never missed a day at the mill –
except for the years between 1956 and 1963 when it
was shut after frost had ruined the olive crops. If
ever one were needed, he would surely be the best
advertisement possible for this wholesome, thick,
deep golden 'oil of the country'.

34. Sunset Sepulchres
at St. Roman

On the way back from the oil mill at Beaucaire we
had a great stroke of luck. It was a beautiful, still
evening, so we decided to climb up to the ruined
Abbey of St. Roman which spectacularly crowns a
hill three kilometres outside the town. Each time
we've passed there until now there has either been a

crushing, *cigale*-enchanted heat, or a freezing Mistral-chilled cold. But this time conditions were all that could be desired, so up we went following the rough track winding round through the thick maquis until we reached the breathtaking viewpoint.

The horizon was uninterrupted from the Cévennes to the Luberon, from Avignon to Arles and beyond. Below, like some coloured *papier-mâché* project, stretched the Rhône obediently tamed into passing the Vallabrègues dam, while the usual thunder of these falling waters was represented only by a small flecked line of white across the river.

Through tangled bushes we entered the strange ruin, or, rather, the superimposed confusion of remains constructed in, on, and under the rock. The only printed description we'd previously read had mentioned the fifteenth century but the curious mixture of ogival arches with stretches of rude rock ceiling in the former church, left us in astonishment.

'I wonder however many periods of architecture it includes,' said Fernand, 'and which would be the oldest.'

'Fifth century,' came a decisive and totally unexpected reply.

We turned in surprise and the speaker explained that, although from the north of France, he was a member of the Archaeological Society at Beaucaire and had spent all his recent holidays working on the excavations of St. Roman. The greater part of the restorations so far achieved have been done by this group of amateurs, including several young people. And now here was one of their most knowledgeable members offering to guide us round – a stroke of luck indeed.

'Yes,' he continued, 'and this extraordinary throne, carved in the stone of the transept here, is a rare and excellent example of the Carlovingian era. It must, of course, have been the Abbatial Seat.'

He sighed and added, 'But so much is necessarily supposition. The choir would have been there, but whose was this tomb of honour beside the altar? I was here when it was found. We know from the Archives that there were two important silver reliquaries in the Abbey, one containing a foot of St. Trophime, but so far we've found no reference to show who was buried here.

'Almost certainly he was recognized as a Saint, for these openings on each side would have been used for passing through objects to touch the body – and there, in the ceiling, is what seems to be an orifice to enable the tomb to be seen from a chapel above. Possibly this was arranged when the Abbot was Guillaume de Grimoard, better known as Urban V, the fourteenth-century Pope who tried to return the papacy from Avignon to Rome.'

I vaguely remembered that Urban had given help to Oxford University and our new friend corroborated. 'Yes, indeed, and it was because he was such a great patron of learning that he founded a college here for the youths of Tarascon and Arles. The Abbey was then at the height of its influence, with perhaps a hundred monks, but the College, or Studium, had a secular as well as religious curriculum.

'The building was above this church but, before we go up there, notice this primitive chapel which perhaps was the cell of the first hermit to settle here;

and this other one with the ceiling blackened by fire; these holes for the oil lamps; the crosses cut in the walls; this stone-scooped holy-water stoup; and everywhere these tombs.'

In this way our voluntary guide made the ruins come alive and we began to notice features which we'd almost certainly have otherwise overlooked. Fernand even spotted the beginnings of a column which had not yet been remarked by our mentor.

We clambered up among the rubble above the church and past more recently discovered tombs dug in the rock-face. Some were so small that they must have been for children. Could some of the College boys have died up here, far above their respective towns? Or, more likely, did the monks have certain small children under their care in the monastery? In any case, some of these shorter tombs were used for transferring old bones, so that the full-length sepulchres could be used again. Isolated tombs here must have been those of the hermit members of the Community, for, although following the Benedictine rule, many were attracted to the ideals of the desert monks of the East as preached by the fifth-century St. Roman.

The full title of this Abbey is St. Roman de l'Aiguille, due to the needle-shaped pinnacle of rock just across from the main buildings. There, too, the hermits settled, and still more on the other neighbouring summit known as the Roche Triple Levée.

Did St. Roman himself found the abbey? It is possible. If not, certainly it was one of his disciples. In 1102 it was noted as already being very old; and a century later Raymond VI granted all the lands around to the monastery. We visited some of the former rock cells, where remains of cupboards can still be seen. Above one doorway is an inscription in Latin: 'Vitalis lived in this modest Cell,' and our archaeologist friend told us that this was likely to have been the thirteenth-century Vitalis mentioned in the Archives as having been pursued by the youths of Tarascon from whom he had saved a woman.

The fresh water spring which must have existed no longer flows but the system of wells, water storage and canalization is still in place. This would have been developed in the sixteenth century when the monastery was secularized and transformed into a fortified castle.

By 1537 the numbers of the monks had dwindled and they arranged an exchange with one François de Conseil, who owned a sizable house at Aigues-Mortes. Thither the community retired, leaving François to install himself and his family in the secularized abbey on top of this barbarous hill. The big paving stones and the so-called Grand Salle – once three separate buildings – are about all that remain of this castle. Those and the famous window from which François' unfortunate son, Nicolas, fell to his death on August 2nd, 1574, while trying to escape during the wars of religion.

Because an official inquiry took place into this death, posterity is informed at least about this moment of St. Roman's history. The former Abbey had a remarkably strategic position during these religious wars, not only being high but also being placed mid-way between Protestant Nîmes and Catholic Provence. Nicolas could therefore judge which side was temporarily the stronger and he adjusted his sights accordingly, inviting first one party and then the other to his castle.

However, he soon found that life with a garrison of either Catholics or Protestants was intolerable and he made elaborate arrangements for getting rid of the occupying soldiers. With great precaution he gradually gathered his friends from Beaucaire and the region, admitting them in ones and twos, until they outnumbered the garrison. Then, at a given moment, when all the soldiers were out on the hill, Nicolas slammed the barbican shut from inside. Alas for him, one soldier proved still to be within. Nicolas shot at him and missed, so that the man was able to let his comrades enter.

Needless to say, the inmates of the castle were then hotly pursued by the soldiers and it was then that Nicolas met his death. Perhaps he was trying to be too cautious, for apparently it was the covers which he had knotted together that gave way and caused the fall. Or, maybe, he was unlucky where he landed; for one of his companions from Montfrin jumped without trying for support, rolled down the hillside and made his way home to tell the tale.

It is said that each subsequent night of August 2nd Nicolas's phantom walks the ruins but a group of young people who this year dared the nocturnal noises and solitude of the place did not succeed in meeting him.

We walked back across the flagstones, past two storage chambers and a half-excavated wall showing clearly vestiges of the three main eras of the building's history – monastery, school and castle. Following Nicolas's death St. Roman passed through the hands of several well-known families in the area but at the time of the Revolution most of the rafters were sold, causing ruin to set in irrevocably. Finally, about 1850, Monsieur Raousset of Boulbon to whom the ex-abbey then belonged (and incidentally whose family, you may remember, once owned our Mas) decided to pull the rest down in order to avoid paying the exorbitant door and window taxes' on a building which gave him no return.

'So much is known but so much is still supposition,' again lamented our friend. 'For so much information was buried with the occupants of the tombs.'

Alone, or in twos and threes, these graves now lie revealed; some were hidden under the trees and bushes which have long since invaded the precincts. Many contained bones and some entire skeletons.

'And look at this,' said the archaeologist, with the flourish of a compère producing the best of the bill, and we stepped across a low wall to stop, stupefied.

There, stretched across the slope of the hill lay row upon row of white, rock-hewn sepulchres.

'Eleventh, twelfth and thirteenth centuries intermingled. Obviously the main cemetery of the monastery. Many of the skulls found are now down at our headquarters.'

The wind whispered gently in the pines behind as the setting sun's reflection illuminated these rediscovered tombs. It was an unforgettable sight.

Later, we called at the headquarters of the Archaeological Society in Beaucaire to see the skulls and to meet the young President of these men who seek to change supposition into known history. Everything he told us about their finds in the district was interesting but, for me at least, the greatest impact of their work remained the picture of that stretch of sunset sepulchres at the Abbey of St. Roman de l'Aiguille.

35. Plumbing Problems and a Corner of Vaucluse

Provençal plumbing is not infrequently precarious. Our present problem is simply one of a cracked bidet and an unobtainable plumber, but we were recently spending a few days with a friend when her lavatory pan suddenly started making a curious Glug-glug noise if flushed. After various abortive attempts to find the plumber, we eventually ran him to earth at the lunch table surrounded by young progeny. Our friend put him in a good humour by remarking that he looked as young as the eldest son and then told him about the noise.

'It goes Glug-glug,' he repeated in understandable astonishment.

We assured him it did and he promised to Come and Look. For days nothing happened and then one morning, while we were all still in bed, he arrived. He pulled the plug as we all listened anxiously.

'Unmistakably it goes Glug-glug,' he agreed, looking perplexed and repeating the performance twice more.

He cocked his head on one side the better to hear the Glug and stared fixedly at the gurgling water for inspiration. We waited in respectful silence for the master-mind's pronouncement and at last it came.

'If it goes Glug-glug like that it's not a plumber

you need,' he said, slowly straightening up. 'It's the *Fosse Septique* that causes that. What you need is a builder.'

No sooner had he gone out of sight down the lane than the hot-water system gave a sigh and went out. By the time we got to the village, the plumber was out again too. However, his son came, swept the machine with a glance and said briefly, 'Need to change the part, have to go to Beaucaire.'

Now, in the first place, Beaucaire is seventeen kilometres away from our friend's house and, in the second place, parts to be obtained have a habit of taking weeks, or even months, en route. We accordingly resigned ourselves not only to the Glug-glug until a builder could be found but also to boiling endless kettles of water; and, to cheer the situation, decided to go out for the rest of the day into the neighbouring department of the Vaucluse.

One of the really astonishing things about Provence is the variety of scenery, agriculture and habits within short distances. The Gard is of course not really Provence, but it is only just across the river and the background and outlook of the people is so different from those here in the Bouches du Rhône. In the other direction, much of the Var is comparatively wild and barren; while the Vaucluse, too, has many differences. Perhaps it is the effect of its higher hills that sometimes cause the people of the Vaucluse to seem more closed in on themselves.

We drove by way of Carpentras towards the lower slopes of Mont Ventoux and had a lazy picnic there while revelling in the wind-brushed, brown-tinted sweep of countryside opposite. In the valley a lone man ploughed brown furrows with the peaceable rhythm of the old-fashioned, mule-trodden way. Brown vine stumps dotted the rising ground towards the dark twin towers and walls of the Renaissance castle of Le Barroux. And, way beyond and above, the brown gave way to purply-blue to mark the jagged peaks of the Dentelles de Montmirail.

In fact our route was to lead across this range but first we spent a little time in sleepy Malaucène. For, despite the fact that a heavy volumn of traffic now roars through this little town, it still retains a somnolent air, with shutters closed long past the heat of the day.

Malaucène is proud of the fact that Clement V lived there at the beginning of the fourteenth century. It is not, after all, every small place that has a church constructed by a Pope. The narrow back alleys which mount to the Calvary have changed little since these days and even the women rubbing their washing at the public lavoir in the shade of the stately old plane trees have more in common with the fourteenth than the twentieth century. What wouldn't they give for a hot water system that worked even a few days of the year!

After that we bounced up a narrow road, climbing, climbing all the way towards those Dentelles, past places with such intriguing names as Suzette and Beaumes-de-Venise, which is a favourite holiday spot. We'd hoped to visit the chapel of Notre-Dame D'Aubune but it is not permanently open to the public and there was no time to begin a key-hunt just then, as the principal destination of the day was to be Séguret.

Séguret is a real end-of-the-road village, as the route, having ground its way up a steepish hill onto a precarious plateau, gives out completely. Village life is apparently also giving out, for as an old man who was carefully tending his lettuces (growing with difficulty on a rocky terrain) said, 'All the young folk are moving down to the plain. Life's too hard for them here on the hill.' He shook his head in sad resignation and concluded, 'The village is dying.'

Doubtless it is true that his Séguret is no longer what it was but it is far from dying, only changing. For Séguret is an artist's lure and as one passes under the archway and wanders through narrow streets leading to the twelfth-century church, there is plenty of evidence of a new life springing up in Séguret. Moreover the now well-established Festival of Provençal Theatre held here in August does much to consolidate this.

Another end-of-the-road village snuggled at the foot of the Dentelles is Gigondas, so famous for its vineyards, which we passed on the way home. Here, too, the artistic influence is strong, and this year an outstanding one-day Festival of Modern Music and Art was held.

The Saints Cosmas and Damien are Patrons of this village so justly famous for its rich, ruby-red, velvet-smooth wine. It is thought that Roman soldiers may first have brought Gigondas this devotion to the two martyrs, whose statues attract attention in the Romanesque church. There is also a painting of them in the older hillside chapel.

We were surprised by evening falling; for the lantern lit streets and illuminated ramparts and ruins of the castle built by William of Orange cause the village to be transformed in true fairy-tale style. But even greater was our surprise on eventually returning to the house to find the hot-water system

fully restored. The part had been personally
fetched from Beaucaire and immediately installed
by the plumber's son. Who says there are
problems with plumbing in Provence?

36.   *Strikes and the Luberon*

One-day strikes have become quite a feature of
present-day life in France. Agricultural discontent
apart, the people of Provence rarely get particularly
involved in the political disturbances and protest
meetings generally organized during a strike.
Instead, they more usually go peaceably fishing, or
shooting, down to the sea, or up to the hills – according to season. So when there was a one-day strike of
small shopkeepers while we were staying with our
friend, we decided to follow the trend and go out for
the day.

Unfortunately, however, it hadn't occurred to us
that small shopkeepers could also include small garage owners; with the result that no petrol was to be
had in our area. As is so often the way if you want
information, there seemed to be nobody about, but
at last, on the road outside St. Rémy, we met an
individual and stopped to ask if he knew where
petrol might be obtained. He pushed his cap back,
scratched his ear, shifted his cigarette-stub and said,
'The bakers are open.'

'Cars don't run on bread, you fat-head,' called a

woman from a window. 'They say the B.P. is open at St. Etienne-du-Grès.'

For once 'they' proved right, so with tank filled we headed for another, less trafficked, corner of the Vaucluse – the long line of hills known as the Luberon.

It is a strange, sometimes sinister-seeming area. I don't know whether it's because of the deep, cold shadows compared with our longer sun-filled hours; or because of reading the horrible history of the Luberon massacres of Protestants; or just because one feels the mystery of the lengthy and largely undelved past of this region of scattered population and the dry stone *'boris'* of still uncertain origins – whatever the reason, the Luberon never quite seems to belong to the otherwise smiling face of Provence.

This sense of eeriness fell most strongly as we were driving down the tortuous little road between Saignon and Buoux. It came as a definite relief to us all to emerge from a ravine, able once more to see the surrounding countryside and look past the solitary bell-tower of a ruined priory towards the ancient fort of Buoux, or further back towards Saignon.

Saignon, by contrast, is sufficiently high and open to avoid giving this sense of oppression and we had had an agreeable picnic in one of the fields which in spring are thick with tiny narcissi. From here the panorama extended from Ventoux to the Lower Alps, and the contrasting shapes of these hills against a sky of curiously variegated clouds, caused the artists among us to whip out blocks and pencils, paints and paper. Meanwhile Saignon is a village worth exploring, with a Romanesque church and the ruins of a fortress founded by the Romans, rebuilt for later use and now abandoned to tenacious gilly-flowers which blossom in every crevice.

But to return to our route after Buoux, we climbed to the edge of the Massif des Cèdres (which divides the Great and Little Luberon, and where fossils of prehistoric mammals have been found) to look down towards the impressive castle of Lourmarin. A mingle of Middle Ages and Renaissance, it was restored at the beginning of this century and is now used as a combined museum, conference centre and concert hall. Then, from picture-postcard Bonnieux, we could clearly see as far as Gordes and red-earthed Roussillon; while on a promontory in the foreground rose all that remains of the former castle of the Marquis of Sade.

Down in the less austere surroundings of Ménerbes, we called on a friend whose house is packed straight into the side of the hill, and so gives a remarkable perspective of the rock-encased village. Ménerbes was once a fortified city and the last stronghold of the Calvinists. Fifteen months' siege was necessary before they were forced to leave.

From the walls we looked across towards the half-ruined village of Oppède-le-Vieux, which was one of twenty-five places sacked by order of François I in 1545, because the inhabitants stubbornly insisted on belonging to the sect of the Vaudois. More than 2,000 people were hung or tortured to death: only the able-bodied men being spared for fuel for the galleys.

Ménerbes has remained surprisingly intact considering the number of times the fortress changed hands during the wars of religion: the stronger party temporarily being installed inside, while the weaker camped without. Even in these days there has been a good deal of changing over between parties of different nationalities. While looking at the scars and lamenting the wounds of the Luberon, we couldn't help remarking the ironical situation that in the face of the strike everybody was levelled for at least one day by their inability to buy anything at all in the shops – except bread.

But were we right? Maybe it was for them as for us just a question of knowing the right person at the right moment. For when we returned and passed a small shop whose owner we all knew well, lo and behold, it was open all the time. All day long the owner had sat with shutters closed, for fear of the Syndicat.

'But nobody,' she said, 'can stop me from obliging my friends in need.' She winked and added conspiratorially, 'Don't just look at the shutters, try the doors and you'll find I'm not the only one.'

37. *Wind-buffeted Hill*

Armed with piles of warm clothing, we set off yesterday afternoon to climb Mont Ventoux – in the car, of course, unlike Petrarch, who was one of the first people to reach the summit on foot more than 600 years ago. Ventoux means 'wind-buffeted' and this 1,912-metre hill is famous for the raging gales which batter its exposed summit, causing the temp-

erature there to be on average eleven degrees cen-
tigrade less than in the valleys below. Terrible tales
are recounted by people who either from necessity
or foolhardiness venture to the peak when the Mistral blows.

We crossed the River Durance (and therefore
from the Bouches du Rhône into the Vaucluse once
more) at Bonpas and, after disentangling its con-
fusing network of arterial roads, headed for
Pernes-les-Fontaines. From 968 Pernes was the
capital of the Comtat Venaissin until it ceded to
Carpentras in 1320; but its most attractive archway, of Notre Dame, and the Fountain of the
Cormorant are both Renaissance.

After Carpentras and Malaucène we turned up
the road past the paper mills towards the Spring and
Chapel of Grozeau. Doubtless it was due to the
spring that Benedictine monks settled here in the
fourteenth century and were often visited by Pope
Clement V when he was at Malaucène. And maybe
the same spring had already had a mystical significance in the pagan mind, for the chapel is almost
certainly built over the remains of a former temple.
Nowadays it is a camping site which benefits from
the cool, clear water.

The tents once left behind, the scenery
immediately takes on the aspect common to all
mountainous regions, so that the route hair-pins
among terraced ground, then rocks with clinging
pines. Thyme creeps low between the cedars and
oaks, while the Forest of Malaucène gives place to
the Forest of Beaumont of Ventoux. As we climbed
higher, the red leaves and berries of early autumn
tinted the way to the first view-point, where the air
was already noticeably fresher. Fernand was more

courageous than I in looking down to the sheer drop below.

Ears were popping by the time we were 1,450 metres high beside the chalets of Mt. Serein, but St. John's Wort, Ragged Robin and many kinds of the Umbelliferae family were still growing in the lush grass under the trees. There was little traffic apart from the tractors loaded with manure from the cows brought here for summer pasturage.

Snow barricades took the place of the trees and we were driving to the summit through the myriad off-white stones, which, sunlit and from a distance, often give a false impression that Ventoux is covered by snow even during summer. A few small pines struggled for existence in this wilderness of scattered stone almost to the foot of the tall, white and red striped television tower, which points like a space-capsule to the sky. Beside this is the meteorological station and two large air-force radar screens.

Indifferent to all this modernity, two ravens croaked above the hotel-restaurant, whose presence would perhaps have shocked Petrarch the most. The date of his great ascent was May 9th, 1336, and in 1936 the French Alpine Club had the nice thought of placing a commemorative tablet on which is inscribed: 'My inviolate summit and my barren, abrupt sides, were first described and poetically sung by François Petrarch, lover of Laura and hermit of the Vaucluse, who united the restoration of ancient letters to the first assertion of alpine literature.'

Another engraved stone nearby recalls the Professor F. Leenhardt who from 1875 to 1883 studied Mont Ventoux and presented the first geological map of the hill. But today's tourist is generally more interested in looking at the view and experiencing the thrill of the buffeting wind. On a clear day one can see from Marseille to Mont Blanc and from the Cévennes to the Italian frontier. The day we were there was far from clear but people none the less were putting coins into the telescope through which they stared at the distant blurred shapes of mountains enshrouded in the thick mist.

But far stranger than the mist was the complete lack of wind. On any hill of this height it would have been remarkable enough, but on the hill called Wind-Buffeted it was unbelievable. So unbelievable that, although all the rest of us were strolling about in cotton frocks or shirt sleeves, one lady insisted not only on wearing her layers of thick sweaters but also in clutching a long woollen scarf ready for the moment the ferocious wind would blow.

Having mounted by the north face, we descended by the south, where at first the stones lie so thickly as to give the effect of an undulating beach. As the people on the top became pin-points, we came level with the memorial to the Englishman, Tom Simpson, who died here during the Tour de France.

A group of people standing disconsolately by the dry Fontaine de la Grave had to decide whether to go on up to the summit, now looking like some distant desert, or down to the ski-centre of Chalet Reynard for their drink. The sight of a taxi heading upwards encouraged them to follow, while we went on through the Forest of Bedoin, where black pines and cedars mingle with elms, evergreen oaks and oaks of the ordinary variety. Underfoot was blue with thistles and dwarf lavender. When it rains, this is a paradise for mushroom hunters, who come from far to search for the fungi.

We used the cement-grooved, slanting, sharp corner of St. Estève, obligatory for drivers engaged in the Course de Ventoux, although a gentler tarmac bend has been constructed for tourists, and suddenly found ourselves back, as it were, in normal Provence at the little hamlet of Les Bruns, where the cicadas were singing in the pines surrounding the cherry trees, figs and vines. This impression of home-coming was heightened by the name of the next tiny village: Les Baux, where the earth was almost the same colour as that surrounding Les Baux near St. Rémy, which, as you know, gave its name to bauxite. But then we were in Bedoin, which is surveyed by an old, fortress-like church with its iron-caged bell-tower; but also possesses a most up-to-date building for its Mairie, as well as a stadium and swimming-pool.

After Bedoin came the cornfields of Montmoiron, as we turned left for Villes-sur-Auzon through scenery opening out into softly rounded, tree-clad hills. Villes-sur-Auzon is called the Gateway of the Gorges de la Nesque, and the pretty road which winds up from there above the ravines has been made even more attractive by the efforts of the men responsible for trimming the hedges. Instead of just cutting back the branches, they have taken the trouble for mile after mile to prune every bush possible into decorative shapes.

The Gorges de la Nesque are a gentler version of the Gorges du Tarn – without the multitude of tourists – and without water. Where was the Nesque? At every turn we expected to see at least a rivulet running in the depths between the rocks; or splashing down the sides of a gully; but at every turn all remained waterless as far as the eye could see, both below and into the blue distance.

After passing several times through walls of rock, the route reached the view-point opposite the massive Rocher du Cire, which certainly does have the appearance of dripping wax. In 1966 the Félibrige co-operated with the municipality of Sault to erect a slab here commemorating the centenary of Frédéric Mistral's 'Calendau', in which he wrote of this Rocher du Cire that no cat or goat or satyr had ever climbed it – 'and never will'.

Far behind, Ventoux now seemed less gaunt and more like an elongated part of the hillside where we stood – as indeed geologically it is. By the road was a shut-up Mas, one of extremely few habitations to be met along the whole of this route. The first real signs of life come from Monieux, with its needle like piece of castle perched on the side of the hill. Here were cows and beehives, and goats in clover; and here too began the lavender fields of Haute Provence. Before we even saw the flowers we smelt them, for Monieux's small lavender distillery was working full tilt.

Sault, too, next town en route has its distillery, so that the air between these two places was heavily perfumed. From the highest pass above the Gorges de la Nesque, Sault appears to be low-lying but once one is down in the plain the town rears high above on a rocky promontory.

From there we crossed the Plateau de Vaucluse, among the purple seas of lavender, to drive down past the sheep beside the castle of Javon and then follow a broom-brushed road by-passing Lioux and red Roussillon to the left, and Joncas mounted to

the right. By the foot of the Gordes' escarpment
long-haired goats browsed among fennel, oblivious
of the view across to the implacable, grey line of the
Luberon opposite.

Past Cabrières with its cedar-forest we aimed for
Cavaillon, to cross the Durance once more with
noses set first for the Alpilles and finally for the
Montagnette. From there we looked back for the
last time at the mass of Mont Ventoux – that Wind-
Buffeted Hill – and the laugh was surely on us as we
emptied the car of all those extra wind-proof
clothes.

38. *Provençal Pilgrimage*

Pilgrimages have an important place in Provençal
life. For the most part they are traditional thanks-
givings, in accordance with a vow made by the ances-
tors of the villagers concerned. So September this
year saw the 250th procession by the people of
Noves in honour of St. Roch, whose intercession
had saved their forefathers from the plague. And
the end of August found the folk of Maillane being
faithful to the vow made by the village elders 117
years ago to remember the deliverance of their village from cholera after prayers to Notre Dame des
Graces. But, of course, you know all about both
these processions from my descriptions in the past.

Another, and even older, pilgrimage touched us
more immediately when we lived in Tarascon near
the Gateway of St. Jean. It is there that the towns-

people take charge of the statue of Notre Dame du Château brought eight kilometres from the village of St. Etienne-du-Grès on every fifth Sunday after Easter. For the following forty days the statue stays in the church of St. Martha at Tarascon and is then returned for the rest of the year to the twelfth-century chapel which stands on the side of the Alpilles above the Roman road at St. Etienne. This again concerns a history of escape from the plague in the Middle Ages; while the pilgrimage to Notre Dame du Bon Remède at Frigolet dates even further back to the tenth-century cures of malaria.

However, last Sunday we joined one of the most important Provençal pilgrimages and one whose origins at least were not connected with diseases. Moreover this is no one-day affair but continues throughout September and has a Grand Pardon attached – similar to those of Brittany. For this is the pilgrimage in honour of St. Gens, youthful prophet to whom the people would not listen. Having thus offended God, they wanted to offer reparation, and so the custom of the pilgrimage began.

St. Gens was born at the beginning of the twelfth century in the small town of Monteux, situated in the Comtat Venaisson (which is now engulfed in the department of the Vaucluse). According to the story, the people of Monteux were extremely superstitious, as indeed a lot of people in Provence still are. Also they frequently lacked rain, as most people in Provence still do. So they had thought up the idea of immersing a statue of St. Raphael in the river on his feast day, with the express aim of annoying the Archangel so much that by way of vengeance he would cause Monteux to be inundated with rain.

St. Gens, although still only a young boy, tried to point out that not only was this practice plainly ridiculous but also pagan. Needless to say, his interference was not well received and life soon became impossible for him in Monteux, so one day he left home, driving before him the two cows with which he used to work the fields.

So we, too, passed through Monteux – nowadays famous for its manufacture of fireworks – and followed St. Gens along the way towards Venasque. In fact he didn't ever reach Venasque, because on arrival at St. Didier he felt inspired to turn off to the right in his search for suitable solitude in which to lead a hermit's life.

Between Monteux and Carpentras today the route is purely functional, but afterwards it becomes enjoyable as it moves gently in the direction of the Plateau de Vaucluse. A deep-toned bell was ringing as we came to St. Didier – so called after a Bishop of Venasque who was killed by brigands – but we decided all the same to take the road to the left and visit Venasque itself before catching up with St. Gens.

Planted solidly in rock formations, Venasque surveys all the countryside around and for this reason has held an important place in history. First the Celtic-Ligurians and then the Romans used it to control the route to Apt, but its most influential epoch was between the sixth and tenth centuries when it was the seat of the Bishops, and when it gave its name to the whole of the Comtat Venaisson.

We climbed up and towards the church whose spire rises above the rest of the village like a solitary candle on a cake. For despite its glorious past, Venasque is today just a village; largely rescued from ruin by wealthy outsiders and, like Gigondas, endowed by them with a cultural festival. The attraction in the twelfth-century church is in the second chapel on the left where a primitive painting of the Avignon School, in which egg was mixed with the colours, depicts the Crucifixion in clear-cut detail.

The former sixth-century church lies below this building and in its turn was constructed on a Roman temple. It was in fact no ordinary church but one which incorporated the large Baptistry where the Bishops of Venasque officiated each Easter. The only other Baptistry in France with such large dimensions is at Poitiers, which dates from the fourth century.

Before being immersed for their Baptism, the neophytes had to purify themselves at the thermal spring near the entrance to the building. The two holes through which the water flowed into the trough can still be seen in the wall. There was originally a low wall all round the font, which is, of course, below floor level, and the floor was then covered by brown and black and white mosaics. The hole is not exactly in the middle of the Baptistry as the light used to be reflected to it from a cupola above.

Two windows have now been cut and one leads out onto a small terrace from where there is a wonderful view across to the Plateau de Vaucluse, with Mont Ventoux to the left. Below lies the convent of Notre Dame de Vie where the non-cloistered Carmelites house the tombstone of Boethius, who died in 604. The farm close by was once the Priory of St. Maurice, which belonged at various eras to the Templars, to the Benedictines of Montmajour and to the Charterhouse at Villeneuve-lēs-Avignon.

Back in the Baptistry a local guide was explaining how pottery had originally been placed in the ceiling to control the acoustics, and she went on to point out a Gallo-Roman corn-mill and a Roman altar to Mercury. I asked where they had been found.

'*Ma foi,*' she replied, 'I couldn't say. Whenever people come across anything like that, they bring it here.'

Then the bells ringing for Mass reminded us it was time to continue the way of St. Gens towards Le Beaucet. In fact we'd have found it much easier if we had followed his right turn at St. Didier, because after Venasque there are only hand-written notices vaguely indicating the direction of Le Beaucet –and even they give out.

After meandering under overhanging trees and past field after field of peach trees, we at last met a chasseur who assured us that we were at least going towards Le Beaucet. This must be one of the worst signposted villages in the Vaucluse, but it's not too surprising as there's very little of it left. The last remnants of a castle wall crown a few mostly ruined, but none the less picturesque, houses and a church.

St. Gens drove his two cows three kilometres beyond Le Beaucet before establishing his hermitage at the end of a wild valley now known as the Holy Valley. We followed the gathering pilgrims past two roadside shrines among hazel-bushes yellow tinged for autumn and came to the cul-de-sac where a chapel has been built over the grotto in which the saint sheltered. Like St. Francis, he tamed the wild beasts; to such an extent that when a wolf so far forgot itself as to eat one of the cows, St. Gens caused the animal to take its place working with the rudimentary plough.

Meanwhile, back in Monteux, three years passed without rain and the people began to wish they had listened to St. Gens. His mother set forth to find him and after pausing to pray at the shrine of Notre Dame de Santé in Carpentras eventually found the right path. A small chapel today marks the spot where by tradition she met her son; while a little further on is the spring which St. Gens is said to have caused to spurt from the rock when, feverish with heat, his mother asked for water.

She told him about Monteux and begged him to return to a people more than ready to receive him. To please her he went, but once his prayers had caused the needed rain to fall, the townsfolk turned against him once more. So he went back to his lonely valley, vowing never to leave it again.

He died young and, according to the legend, it was the wolf whose presence in Monteux brought news of its master's death. However that may be, the people finally repented of their behaviour and went in procession to the hermitage, promising to repeat this act of penitence every year. This act of devotion spread throughout Provence until as many as five thousand people have been known to gather for the Grand Pardon of September.

There were not as many as that this year but the chapel was nevertheless packed to standing on the Sunday we were there. A folklore group had come from Carpentras to give a display of dancing during the afternoon, but there were few tourists, the congregation being formed almost entirely of pilgrims. They chanted together in Latin and French, and listened attentively to the sermon in Provençal, in

which the preacher recalled his first pilgrimage to
St. Gens fifty years ago. Almost all received Communion and then climbed up the old stairs leading
past the tomb of St. Gens.

The sick especially looked longingly at the
crutches and other tokens left to indicate cures
which have occurred after prayers for St. Gens'
intercession. The walls are covered with plaques of
thanksgiving by no means all old – one still shining
new was donated in 1970.

After the Mass the gilded reliquary statue, showing St. Gens between the cow and the wolf, was
carried in a procession which everyone joined –
even a blind man who was singing the final canticle
with all his might.

On the way through the trees to the spring we fell
in beside a viticulturist from Orange who had come
on behalf of his neighbour to fetch a bottle of this
water – which many pious people in Provence like to
keep in supply at home in case of need.

Fernand wondered whether one had to drink a
great deal before a fever passed.

'Oh no,' came the reply, 'just a little glass will do.'

He seemed so sure that I inquired if he personally
knew somebody who had been cured.

'Yes,' he replied quite simply. 'One of my own
family. She had a bad and most persistent fever that
no medicine touched; then she drank a glass of this
water while asking for the intercession of St. Gens –
and in the morning she was completely fit and well.'

We asked if he had often made the pilgrimage.

'Oh yes,' he said, 'every year for as long as I can
remember; and I always will.'

An old, bent woman in black and wearing a headscarf against the heat, was making her way slowly up

the rough track towards us. In her hand she carried
an empty bottle which she was going to fill. The
water flows slowly and it takes five minutes to collect
a litre. No matter. It was all part of the patient and
sincere performance which makes this pilgrimage
in honour of St. Gens so genuine and truly
Provençal.

39. Casual Characteristics

You comment on my use of the words 'patient and
sincere' in connection with 'truly Provençal', at the
end of my last letter. Yes, fundamentally I believe
these to be two of the most outstanding characteristics of the person of Provence. Certainly he is
fairly easily sparked off over controversial matters,
but the resultant commotion, if any, rarely has any
deep significance. He will sometimes shout and
swear and wave his arms about, while really being no
more affected than by a passing attack of sneezing.
Basically he, and especially she, is a great acceptor of
events. '*C'est comme ça*' (That's the way of it) and '*Tout
s'arrangera*' (Everything will sort itself out) still sum
up much of the philosophy of Provence.

The Provençal can sometimes appear casual. This
may be that he does not want to become involved,
for he is a fiercely independent individualist. But it
may also just be that he is intent on some other
aspect – such as the harvest, or treatment of crops –

and being a generally single-minded person, he finds it difficult to split his attention.

He hates a lot of palaver and show-off, which appears to him a sign of insincerity. He is essentially natural, simple and shrewd. If he wants to know something, he'll inquire: there is no conception that perhaps it is impolite to ask personal questions. If the stranger answers as directly, he will be on the first step to establishing friendship. The least sign of affectation, standoffishness, or taking umbrage and, although he will be treated correctly by an innately courteous folk, the outsider will never really achieve any real rapport.

'*Il est brave*' is a frequent expression used by one person of the Midi to describe another's character, and in effect it sums up very well all that is best. The word *brave* here has nothing to do with the English brave or courageous. Rather it denotes a gentle willingness to help others, coupled with an unwillingness to cause trouble. Often it includes generosity and the sentence may then be completed by 'and he'd give you the shirt off his back'.

What I am saying particularly applies to the countryfolk, who are less touched by the modern speedy way of life than those in the larger towns – especially the youth – though even in the towns there is generally a far greater readiness to help others than one finds further north.

Another aspect of the Provençal's character is his sense of humour. The Provençal language is full of picturesque and amusing sayings, which of course lose hopelessly in the translation, but this feeling for the *mot juste* and the ability of repartee are carried into the use of French. It is during local gatherings or in the small restaurant such as one we entered the other day, that a free and easy exchange of conversation is often at its best.

Talk intermingled from table to table like that along crossed telephone wires.

'I'm just a simple workman passing my time going up and down,' one young man was explaining earnestly to his companion, when from the table beside came the quick reply, 'In that case, you'd do better to take the lift.'

Everyone is interested in everyone else in these cafés – especially those of the Routiers. Last weekend at Carpentras we collected some most useful addresses of good places to eat from a lorry driver and a man who travelled from market to market throughout France to sell his wares.

It was a long-distance lorry driver who attracted most of the attention. With his blue trousers having trouble to cover a large paunch, and his pullover being tortured by expansive explanatory gestures, he was telling the story of how he was belting along with a trailer carrying a sink, when the coupling came undone and the sink was more than sunk.

Next to catch all ears was a woman recounting how she'd had to answer the telephone for the first time in her life. 'Petrified of the thing, I was,' she was saying, 'and I didn't want to pick it up for not knowing which end to put where. But with all of them looking at me, what could I do but swagger across the room pretending that it was something I did every day.'

'Bravo,' applauded a whiskery man shuffling towards the kitchen in search of more bread. He proved to be a relative of the Patronne, for when he returned he was carrying a bottle of labelled wine and remarked to his table companions, with a broad wink for a larger audience, 'She's only put out the ordinaire.' There were already five bottles of wine on their table but, no matter, the log fire was smoking a bit and that created thirst.

In effect the Provençal generally knows how to take his drink without abusing it and cases of drunkenness are extremely rare. He likes the good things in life in the measure that he can afford them and on festive occasions enjoys himself with the same thoroughness with which he works.

To sum up this collection of rather casual characteristics, I can only go back to the rest of that expression which I used in the previous letter along with 'patient and sincere' – that is 'genuine'. For someone who is genuine is really himself and without side or pretences – and that is truly Provençal.

40. *Looked at and Loved*

It's nearly half a century since E. I. Robson wrote in the book I've already mentioned, *A Wayfarer in Provence*, 'If ever one wanted to learn how to observe (rare faculty!) Provence would be the best of training grounds. To the rushing tourist it can only mean a few hasty impressions and a bundle of picture-post-cards. But our advice is – Travel slow, look at, and love everything.

This continues to hold good today, for despite the fact that inevitably everything now moves at a faster pace, and that there is a lamentable amount of what

Fernand rightly calls 'cinema' in many of the folk-loric displays, there is still that steady rhythm of life in Provence which defies all modernization.

The fever of competition which contaminates the so-called pleasures of relaxation is unknown here. The two principal hobbies of everyday folk are shooting and fishing, but there is no tension about who shoots the most game or catches the biggest fish. More often than not on these Sunday expeditions nothing is shot or caught at all. It is the outing itself that counts; the pleasure of being attuned to nature, and what is largely described as the excuse for 'taking the air'.

Mind you, this laudable desire to take the air can be carried to extremes – and more than once during our fishing expeditions last winter we finished by taking cover rather than oxygen. I particularly recall one day when, despite a bitterly raging Mistral, we set off for one of the two spots where 'there are always fish'. Or so it is said.

While I admit to having seen photographs of outsize pike caught in this stretch of water, I have personally never seen its muddy surface stirred by so much as a minnow. But no matter, following the maxim: If we don't take a fish, we take the air: there we were.

As we stepped out of the car the wind slashed at our faces like the interior of a refrigerator out of control. The reeds were bending with the fervour of modern dance enthusiasts, while ice formed fascinating squares round their stems in the water. Apart from two hawks which showed surprise at the arrival of humans on the frozen scene, there was no sign of anything living. For form's sake, the rods were prepared and four casts made. Then, quick, back to the car with windows shut. Ritual fulfilled; we had 'taken the air'. At the same time we had also seen an aspect of Provence experienced by comparatively few.

The same place on a milder winter's day is full of a charm lost to the crowds who come, transistor in hand, during summer. Robson would find it an ideal training ground for observation. A breeze gently rocks the long lines of reeds, while birds play hide and seek among the thicknesses of stalk. The sun warms the stones sufficiently for sleepy lizards to lie among the tufts of thyme and lavender. On the far side of the stream a black group of bulls graze undisturbed by the cawing rooks. The only other sound except the lapping of the water is the distant intonation of sheep bells from a flock far away behind the Château of Barbegal.

Despite roadworks and river works, there are still a few places comparatively unknown and unfrequented on the banks of the Rhône. One such is in the region of Arles, where at a certain bend in the river one sees the ancient Roman capital of Provence perfectly set in a frame of trees. St. Trophime's tower is just dwarfed by the Mairie to the right, and the spire of St. Mary Major (known always as La Major) to the left beside the cylindrical, high silhouetted Arènes.

Here we can still spend a mid-August afternoon fishing peacefully without entangling the lines in picnickers' bottles and tins. The cigales are not disharmonized by radios; nor are the birds in the tamarisks, the breeze rustling the poplars, nor the rush of the fast-flowing waters of the river. Reeds and wild flowers grow unthreatened by weed-killers, and the swallows (becoming rarer and rarer in Provence) here dart after midges in the still air uncontaminated by insecticides. Two old rowing-boats knock gently together, surrounded by a multitude of dragonflies of all colours and sizes and shapes of wing; while the steady hum of barge motors can be heard long before the vessels come in sight.

Near the Mas is another undisturbed summer fishing haunt with a clear view of the countryside surrounding the Rhône. Before the work began on the Vallabrègues' dam the banks here were wonderfully thick with trees and bushes: now all is bare and access restricted. But looking across the river one forgets the unfortunate scars, as the light changes on the low hills which form a façade for the distant Cévennes. To the left are the villages of Montfrin and Théziers, while away to the right on a clear day one sees the shapes of the Ventoux and the Dentelles de Montmirail rising into the sky. For the most part here we only catch chub or eels, but the tranquillity and beauty of the place more than make amends.

Sea-fishing is generally left for winter or early spring, when the beaches are free from bathers. Formerly there were also many fish in the Rhône where it empties into the sea at St. Louis. There seem to be few left today but there is always that valid reason for 'taking the air'. A short spell casting there gives the opportunity to survey the wide sweep of sea across the Gulf of Fos, once a small port and now the colossal centre of industrialization. For the moment we can still enjoy the sight of small boats coming across to the harbour of St. Louis, and can also observe the efforts of other fishermen. Not least, this spot gives us an occasional excuse for having lunch at a well-hidden restaurant of unpre-possessing exterior and welcoming interior, where the Patron himself, almost invariably dressed in check shirt and cap, serves deliciously fresh sea-food.

Returning from there one day, we stopped to try our luck in the Canal de Bouc. The wind freshened and great white clouds processed leisurely across the sky with the lazy dignity of giant fish in an aquarium; but nothing fishy disturbed the waters below. A chasseur and his dog came over the brow of the hillock behind the canal and stopped to pass the time of day – for there is always a camaraderie among those who meet far from the crowd.

He had shot nothing. We had caught nothing. No matter. We had all not only 'taken the air' but also taken simple pleasure in following a sport for its own sake. Above all, we had 'travelled slow, looked at, and loved everything'.